iPhone Gu

Maximizing the Future of Cell Phone

Technology

Brooke Jade

ISBN: 978-1-63750-216-7

Table of Contents

Introduction

Over-70 million cell phone users in the world especially in United States of America, United Kingdom, Germany, France, Italy, Canada, Australia, India, Spain, Africa and other European countries, African countries, Asian countries and lot more uses the iPhone 7, iPhone 7 Plus, iPhone 8, iPhone 8 Plus, iPhone X, iPhone XR, iPhone XS, iPhone XS Max, iPhone 11 and iPhone 11 aren't just faster and more powerful than ever—they're also better at all of the things you use an iPhone DEVICE for. Following this informative guide, you will get a gorgeously illustrated guide to the shortcuts, tips, and workarounds that will turn you into an iPhone master very fast without much ado.

It helps you accomplish everything from web browsing to watching videos, shooting unique photographs, watching and streaming live TV for FREE, importing and exporting contacts, files, unlocking iPhones, fixing iPhone problems and lot more. You'll get up to speed on features now one talks about which are available on your iPhone devices.

This easy-to-use book will also get you up to speed on all iOS 12 features, including new Siri shortcuts, Group FaceTime, and improved performance features and also makes the information simple enough for kids, adolescents, and adult even if they are dummies, seniors and experts in the computer and technology world...

CHAPTER 1

Getting Started with New iPhone

There is no need connecting your brand-new iPhone to your personal computer, as long as there is a mobile data connection designed for activation. As you end the set-up wizard, you may navigate back by tapping the back arrow at the top left-hand side of the screen and scroll further to another display by tapping another button at the top right-hand corner.

You can commence by pressing down the power button at the top edge of your brand-new iPhone. You may want to keep it pressed down for about two seconds until you notice a vibration, meaning the iPhone is booting up.

Once it boots up finally, you can start initial set up by

following the processes below;

- Swipe your finger over the display screen to start the set-up wizard.

- Choose the language of preference - English is usually at the top of the list, so there is no problem finding it. However, if you would like to apply a different language, scroll down to look for your desired language, and tap to select the preferred language.

- Choose your country - United States may be near the top of the list. If otherwise, scroll down the list and select the United States or any of your choice.

- You need to connect your iPhone to the internet to start its activation. You can test this via a link with a Wi-Fi network. Locate the name of your available network in the list shown, and then tap on it to select it.

- Enter the Wi-Fi security password (you will generally find this written on your router, which is probably known as the WPA Key, WEP Key, or Password) and select Sign up. A tick indication shows you are connected, and a radio image appears near the top of the screen. The iPhone will now start activation with Apple automatically. This may take some time!

- In case your iPhone is a 4G version, you will be requested to check for updated internet configurations after inserting a new Sim card. You can test this anytime, so, for the present time, tap **Continue**.

- Location services will help you with mapping, weather applications, and more, giving you specific information centred wholly on what your location is. Select whether to use location service by tapping allow location services.

- You would now be requested to create **Touch ID,** which is Apple's fingerprint identification. **Touch ID** allows you to unlock your iPhone with your fingerprint instead of your passcode or security password. To set up Tap Identification, put a finger or your thumb on the home button (but do not press it down!). To by-pass this for the moment, tap *setup Tap Identification later*.

- If you are establishing Touch ID, the tutorial instruction on the screen will walk you through the set-up process. Put your finger on the home button, then remove till the iPhone has properly scanned your fingerprint. Whenever your print is wholly scanned, you will notice a screen letting you know that tap recognition is successful. Tap **Continue.**

- You will be requested to enter a passcode to secure

your iPhone. If you create **Touch ID**, you must use a passcode if in any case your fingerprint isn't acknowledged. Securing your computer data is an excellent idea, and the iPhone provides you with several options. Tap password option to choose your lock method.

- You can arrange a Custom Alphanumeric Code (that is a security password that uses characters and figures), a Custom Numeric Code (digit mainly useful, however, you can add as many numbers as you want!) or a 4-Digit Numeric Code (a high old college pin!). In case you didn't install or setup **Touch ID** you may even have an option not to add Security password. Tap on your selected Security option.

- I would recommend establishing a 4-digit numeric code, or Touch ID for security reasons but all optional setup is done likewise. Input your selected Security password using the keyboard.

- Verify your Security password by inputting it again. If the Password does not match, you'll be requested to repeat! If indeed they do match, you'll continue to another display automatically.

At this time of the set-up process, you'll be asked whether you have used an iPhone before and probably upgrading it, you can restore all of your applications and information from an iCloud or iTunes backup by deciding on the best option. If this is your first iPhone, you will have to get it started as new, yet, in case you are moving from Android to an iPhone, you can transfer all your data by deciding and choosing the choice you want.

How to Restore iPhone Back-up from iCloud or iTunes

If you want to restore your iPhone from an iTunes back-up, you may want to connect to iCloud and have the latest version of iTunes installed on it. If you are ready to begin this process, tap **restore** from iTunes back-up on your iPhone and connect it to your personal computer. Instructions about how to bring back your data can be followed on the laptop screen.

In case your old iPhone was supported on iCloud, then follow the instructions below to restore your applications & data to your brand-new device:

- Tap *Restore* from iCloud back-up.

- Register with the Apple ID and Password that you applied to your old iPhone. If you fail to recollect the security password, there's a link that may help you reset it.

- The Terms & Conditions screen will show. Tap the links to learn about specific areas in details. When you are ready to proceed, select **Agree**.

- Your iPhone will need some moments to create your Apple ID and hook up with the iCloud server.

- You will notice a summary of available backups to download. The most up-to-date backup will be observed at the very top, with almost every other reserve below it. If you want to restore from a desirable backup, tap the screen for *all backups* to see the available choices.

- Tap on the back-up you want to restore to start installing.

- A progress bar will be shown, providing you with a demo of the advancement of the download.

When the restore is completed, the device will restart.

- You would see a notification telling you that your iPhone is updated effectively. Tap *Continue*.

- To complete the iCloud set up on your recently restored iPhone, you should re-enter your iCloud (Apple ID) password. Enter/review it and then tap *Next*.

- You'll be prompted to upgrade the security information related to your *Apple ID*. Tap on any stage to replace your computer data, or even to bypass this option. If you aren't ready to do this, then tap *Next* button.

- **Apple pay** is Apple's secure payment system that stores encrypted credit or debit cards data on your device and making use of your iPhone also with your fingerprint to make safe transaction online and with other apps. Select *Next* to continue.

- To *feature/add a card*, place it on a set surface and place the iPhone over it, so the card is put in the camera framework. The credit card info will be scanned automatically, and you will be requested to verify that the details on display correspond with your card. You'll also be asked to enter the *CVV* (safety code) from the personal strip behind the card. If you choose (or the camera cannot recognize your cards), you can enter credit card information by hand by tapping the hyperlink. You could bypass establishing **Apple Pay** by tapping *create later.*

- Another screen discusses *iCloud keychain*, which is Apple's secure approach to sharing your preserved security password and payment information throughout all your Apple devices. You might use *iCloud security code* to validate your brand-new device and import present data, or you might be asked to continue registering your keychain if it's your first Apple device. In case you don't want to share vital data with other devices, you should go to *avoid iCloud keychain* or *don't restore passwords*.

- If you selected to set up your Apple keychain, you'll be notified to either use Security password (the same one you'd set up on your iPhone) or produce a different code. If you're making use of your iCloud security code, you should put it on your iPhone when prompted.

- This will confirm your ID when signing on to an iCloud safety code; a confirmation code will be delivered via SMS. You may want to hyperlink your smartphone text code (if you have never distributed one with Apple already) so that the code may be provided as a text. Then enter this code to your iPhone if requested, then select *Next.*

- You'll then be asked to create **Siri**. *Siri* is your own digital personal associate, which might search the internet, send communications, and check out data in your device and a lot more, all without having to flick via specific apps. Choose to create Siri by tapping the choice or start Siri later to skip this task for now.

- To set up and create SIRI, you will need to speak several phrases to the iPhone to review your conversation patterns and identify your voice.

- Once you say every term, a tick will be observed, showing that it's been known and comprehended. Another phrase may indicate that you should read aloud.

- Once you've completed the five phrases, you will notice a display notifying that Siri has been set up correctly. Tap *Continue*.

- The iPhone display alters the color balance to help make the screen show up naturally under distinctive light conditions. You can switch this off in the screen settings after the iPhone has completed configuring it. Tap *continue* to continue with the setup.

- Has your iPhone been restored? Tap begin to transfer your computer data to your brand-new iPhone.

- You'll be prompted to ensure your brand-new iPhone has enough power to avoid the device turning off in the process of downloading applications and information. Tap **OK** to verify this recommendation.

- You will notice a notification show up on your apps, to download in the background.

How to Move Data From Android

Apple has made it quite easy to move your data from a Google Android device to your new iPhone. Proceed to the iOS app. I'll direct you about how to use the application to move your data!

- Using the iPhone, if you are on the applications & data screen of the set-up wizard, tap *move data from Google android*.

- Go to the Play Store on your Google android device and download the app recommended by the set-up wizard. When it is installed, open up the app, select **Continue** and you'll be shown the *Terms & Conditions* to continue.

- On your Android device, tap *Next* to start linking your Devices. On your own iPhone, select *Continue*.

- Your iPhone will show a 6-digit code which has to be received into the **Google android** device to set the two phone up.

- Your Google android device will screen all the data that'll be moved. By default, all options are ticked - so if there could be something you don't want to move, tap the related collection to deselect it. If you are prepared to continue, tap *Next* on your Google android device.

- As the change progresses, you will notice the iPhone display screen changes, showing you the position of the info transfer and progress report.

- When the transfer is completed, you will notice a confirmation screen on each device. On your Android Device, select *Done* to shut the app. On your own iPhone, tap *Continue Installing iPhone*.

- An Apple ID allows you to download apps, supported by your iPhone and synchronize data through multiple devices, which makes it an essential account you should have on your iPhone! If you have been using an iPhone previously, or use iTunes to download music to your laptop, then you should have already become an Apple ID user. Register with your username and passwords (when you have lost or forgotten your Apple ID or password you will see a link that may help you reset it). If you're not used to iPhone, select doesn't have an Apple ID to create one for free.

- The Terms & Conditions for your iPhone can be seen. Please go through them (tapping on more to study additional info), so when you are done, tap *Agree*.

- You'll be asked about synchronizing your data with iCloud. That's to ensure bookmarks, connections and other items of data are supported securely with your other iPhone's data. Tap *merge* to permit this or *don't merge* if you'll have a choice to keep your details elsewhere asides iCloud.

- **Apple pay** is Apple's secure payment system that stores encrypted credit or debit cards data on your device and making use of your iPhone also with your fingerprint to make safe transaction online and with other apps. Select *Next* to continue.

- To *feature/add a card*, place it on a set surface and place the iPhone over it, so the card is put in the camera framework. The credit card info will be scanned automatically, and you will be requested to verify that the details on display correspond with your card. You'll also be asked to enter the *CVV* (safety code) from the personal strip behind the card. If you choose (or the camera cannot recognize your cards), you can enter credit card information by hand by tapping the hyperlink. You could bypass establishing **Apple Pay** by tapping *create later*.

- Another screen discusses *iCloud keychain*, which is Apple's secure approach to sharing your preserved security password and payment information throughout all your Apple devices. You might use *iCloud security code* to validate your brand-new device and import present data, or you might be asked to continue registering your keychain if it's your first Apple device. In case you don't want to share vital data with other devices, you should go to *avoid iCloud keychain* or *don't restore passwords*.

- If you selected to set up your Apple keychain, you'll be notified to either use Security password (the same one you'd set up on your iPhone) or produce a different code. If you're making use of your iCloud security code, you should put it on your iPhone when prompted.

- This will confirm your ID when signing on to an iCloud safety code; a confirmation code will be delivered via SMS. You may want to hyperlink your smartphone text code (if you have never distributed one with Apple already) so that the code may be provided as a text. Then enter this code to your iPhone if requested, then select *Next.*

- You'll then be asked to create **Siri**. *Siri* is your own digital personal associate, which might search the internet, send communications, and check out data in your device and a lot more, all without having to flick via specific apps. Choose to create Siri by tapping the choice or start Siri later to skip this task for now.

- To set up and create SIRI, you will need to speak several phrases to the iPhone to review your conversation patterns and identify your voice.

- Once you say every term, a tick will be observed, showing that it's been known and comprehended. Another phrase may indicate that you should read aloud.

- Once you've completed the five phrases, you will

notice a display notifying that Siri has been set up correctly. Tap *Continue*.

- The iPhone display alters the color balance to help make the screen show up naturally under distinctive light conditions. You can switch this off in the screen settings after the iPhone has completed configuring it. Tap *continue* to continue with the setup.

- Has your iPhone been restored? Tap begin to transfer your computer data to your brand-new iPhone.

- You'll be prompted to ensure your brand-new iPhone has enough power to avoid the device turning off in the process of downloading applications and information. Tap *OK* to verify this recommendation.

- You will notice a notification show up on your apps, to download in the background.

NB: *Setting up as new iPhone: Similar method, as described above, applies.*

CHAPTER 2

How to Add Contact to Your iPhone Manually

We have discussed uploading your contacts from your previous device; however, when you begin using your device, you will want to add contacts as you go and edit or update the info of individuals you already have. Don't worry; you will become familiar with that now.

How to Add a New Contact

To include a completely new contact on your iPhone, follow the instructions described below:

- Tap on the Contact App on your home Display.

- You might see any previously existing contacts on your display. To include a brand-new contact, select the blue+ at the very top right-hand nook.

- Enter the name of your brand-new contact in the areas supplied near the top of the screen. To add a mobile number, tap **add mobile**. Tap where it says Telephone to input the number, and you'll change the label home to a choice of yours by tapping it and selecting your desired from a list. To include an electronic email address, tap add E-mail, so that as you scroll down, you might see areas for additional input information, comprising home address, birthday, or even established custom ringtones and message shades for the contact.

- If you are satisfied with the info you have in your brand-new contact, tap *completed* at the very top right-hand nook to save the contact.

- Tap All Contacts at the very top left-hand nook to go again to your contact list.

Once you have stored your contact, select + to feature or add every other or tap the home button to come back to your home screen.

How to Edit iPhone Contact

Editing a contact on your iPhone isn't expected to vary from including a new one, just can be seen barely in yet another way.

To edit a contact:

- Open up the Contacts application from the home display.

- Please scroll down and select the contact you want to edit, to open up it.

- At the very top right-hand corner, tap *Edit*.

- Now you can edit the contact's details as explained above, adding or changing the info as required. If you want to delete any data from a contact, select the pink group icon left of the sphere and tap delete at the right of the range.

- If you wish to delete the contact completely, scroll downwards and select *delete the contact.*

Adding & Importing Contact to Your iPhone

When you have contacts on your old smartphone or device that you'll like to import to your brand-new iPhone, please don't be worried I'll guide you!

Using Apple's iCloud service, you'll be able to import storage space documents and synchronize contacts simultaneously to your iPhone.

If you have formerly been using an iPhone, then transferring your contacts would be more comfortable by using *Apple's iCloud Online Sync Service.*

In case your old mobile device has been installed to use iCloud, then your use of the same Apple identity (ID) on your iPhone will deliver your contacts, calendar, and other information right to your brand-new device with no need for further action.

If you don't have iCloud installed on your old iPhone, then it's the very first thing you will need to configure. Your old iPhone should be associated with a Wi-Fi network so that people can reproduce or duplicate the info from your mobile phone to iCloud.

Do the following on your old iPhone:

- Locate and tap the Configurations icon.

- Scroll down and select *iCloud*.

- If you see your address at the very top line, this means you're authorized directly into iCloud on your old iPhone. If not, subscribe with the same

Apple ID that you've used for your brand-new iPhone.

- Turn internet network **ON.**

- Select the choice to Merge your computer data with **iCloud**. This will add all of your contacts to iCloud.

When you have already passed the initial set up the stage for your iPhone, you might activate the iCloud services following precise instructions as stated above. When you're connected directly to iCloud, your contacts will start to download to your brand-new iPhone immediately. If you have configured your old iPhone to the iCloud service, all you have to do is select the option to use iCloud through the initial set up of your iPhone, as well as your contacts that will automatically show up on these devices.

How to Import Contacts From A Google Android To iPhone

Your Android device can export its contacts into a storage space file, the precise form of a written report which iCloud has is with the capacity of managing and absorbing. Once your links are in iCloud, it is only a matter of time expecting the info to complete synchronizing on your iPhone. However, if you are uncertain how to actualize this stage, then examine the steps below to discover more!

If the contacts aren't on the Google account on your old Android device, we'll need to get them there so that you can transfer these to your iPhone, so that you will need to focus on step one as described below. If the contacts are already in your Google accounts, you may ignore this step.

To migrate your contacts out of your old Android device to your Google accounts:

- On your Android phone, tap the Contacts icon on your home display, or within the programs list.

- Tap the menu key, both as a button below the screen with three lines or the display screen button at the top-right corner, with three dots icon.

- Tap **Import/Export**. Several Android phones need you to press *More* before you start to see the *import/export settings.*

- Tap *Export to SDCARD*, or *Export to Storage Space* depending on your mobile phone.

- When exported and you're back viewing the contacts list, select the *menu key* again.

- Tap *Import/export,* as done in the third step.

- Tap import from **SDCARD** or *import from Storage space* depending on your mobile phone.

- If you are asked where to import the contacts to, tap Google or the Google E-mail address.

- Based on your specific phone, you'll be requested to choose which contacts to import. If so, pick all links. Your links will now be on your Google accounts!

  Given that your contacts are on your Google accounts, you will extract these details and stick it onto the iCloud accounts such that it synchronizes to your iPhone.

- On your laptop, head to Google's contacts website and subscribe with your Google email and password.

- From your Google contact, near the top of your contacts, press *More*, and consequently *Export*.

- Ensure that the all contacts radio field is ticked, in

addition to memory cards format- Press *Export* to download your contacts on your computer.

- From your laptop's web browser, go to the iCloud website and register to make use of your Apple ID and Password.

- Go through the Contacts, a summary of all your contacts presently residing on your iCloud account.

- Press the configurations icon in the bottom-left part of the contacts page. This appears as though it's a cog or tool.

- From your menu which shows up, go through the import button, and navigate to your download folder. After picking your cards to import and Press Okay, your contacts will begin to show in iCloud! Within a few minutes, your iPhone will start to show the same contacts too.

How to Import Contacts From a Blackberry Phone

To control your Blackberry contacts, we first need to transfer these to your computer. To do this, you must first download and set up the blackberry laptop software. As the software is installed, adhere to the instructions below!

- Connect your Blackberry to your laptop by using a micro USB cable for Blackberry processing device computer software to comprehend and identify the smartphone.

- Select Organizer at the left-hand panel of the program and tick the contacts field.

- While requested to choose the Sync Path, choose your laptop/computer only.

- Below contacts account, be sure home windows contacts is chosen. Press **OK** to continue.

- Press sync organizer at the right-hand part of the program to move your Blackberry contacts onto your home windows address book.

- Given that your contacts are saved in windows contacts, you can synchronize these details to your iPhone through the iTunes software. If you have not already installed iTunes, download it from Apple's download website, making sure that your iPhone isn't associated with your personal computer when you install the program.

- If iTunes is currently installed on your pc, connect your iPhone through the provided USB cable and go through the Info Tabs near the top of the summary web page.

- Given that you're at the information tab, you will notice a tick box to Synchronize Your Contacts. Make sure that iTunes is defined to synchronize with your windows contacts; tick the package and press synchronize at the bottom left part of iTunes.

- Your contacts will now be shown on your iPhone! If you have signed directly into iCloud on your mobile phone, your contacts will now start copying to Apple's cloud storage space service.

How to Import Contacts from a Windows Phone

To transfer contacts from a windows phone to your iPhone, you'd first move the contacts to your home windows contacts program on your laptop. That is a reasonably reliable method, and also to learn more, keep reading!

- If you're migrating from a home windows phone and your mobile phone is linked to the internet, you ought to have Home windows Live (or Hotmail) accounts already created on the smartphone. Under these events, your contacts can be stored on the Home windows live website by default. Go through the link and register with your home windows e-mail address and security password when prompted.

- Once you can see your contacts list, click a button near the top of the web page and choose Export from the dropdown list. Your contacts will begin installing as a .csv file on your personal computer.

- On your PC, go through the start menu and open up contacts.

- From the very best of the connection's windows, press import and choose CSV as your selected file type. Press import to save.

- Go through the search button to get the

downloaded duplicate of your home windows live contacts. Once you've located it, press Next to start importing the contacts to your laptop's address folder.

- Given that your contacts are kept in windows contacts, you would be able to synchronize this data to your iPhone through the iTunes program. If you haven't already downloaded iTunes from Apple's download web page, please do.

- If iTunes is currently established on your pc, connect your iPhone via the provided USB cable and go through the *INFO* tabs near the top of the summary web page.

- Given that you're at the info tab, you will notice a tick-box to sync your contacts. Affirm that iTunes is defined to synchronize with your Home windows contacts, tick the field and press

SYNCHRONIZE in the bottom left part of iTunes.

- Your contacts will now show up on your iPhone! If you've signed on directly into iCloud on your mobile phone, your contacts will now start backing up just as much as Apple's cloud storage space service is enabled.

CHAPTER 3

Setting up Mobile Networks & Wi-Fi

Would you like to connect your iPhone to the internet before you begin the utilization of several features, like email and the application store? Right here is a way for connecting your iPhone to a guaranteed wireless network as well as your mobile data network for access to the internet.

You might have recently been linked to Wi-Fi through the preliminary iPhone setup, however, if you didn't, or want to get on a particular wireless network, then this section of the manual is the correct one for you!

Connecting Your iPhone to a Wi-Fi network

For connecting your iPhone to a Wi-Fi network, you'll first need to find the security key for the network. This may be on the sticker at the back or source of your router, and it might be called a WEP Key, WPA Key, or Wi-Fi password. If you're uncertain, you could check up on the person that installs your network, or your web service provider.

When you have this data, you are equipped to start!

- From the home display screen, tap on the configuration's icon.

- Within the settings menu, select *Wi-Fi*.

- Make sure the WiFi switch is preparing to *ON* (green) if it's not from inception, tap the change to *enable/allow* it. Using the WiFi *ON*, your iPhone will check out and screen all available systems. Choose your network's name from the list shown and tap on it.

- When prompted, enter the *Wi-Fi* security password. That is delicate, so be sure you don't mistype it, so when you are ready to continue, tap **Join**.

- When the iPhone is installed to the network, you might visit a blue tick shown up on the network's name, and a radio image will be observed next to your mobile network's name at the very top level of the screen. Whenever your iPhone is at the range of the network, and wireless is switched **ON**, it'll connect automatically.

How to Connect Your iPhone to Mobile Data

If you procure your iPhone on a promo, you might in all

probability have a month data bundle incorporated with the agreement. Allowing you to apply the internet if you are far-away from any Wi-Fi systems. This is set up automatically when you initially start your iPhone, and that means you should manage to connect anywhere as long as there's a stable mobile network transmission strength! If this is not the situation, follow my brief steps below to discover the best way to get the mobile internet ready for use.

- From the home display, Tap on the configuration icon.

- In the predominant configurations listing, tap on Mobile data (depending on your network, you might see Cellular data as an alternative).

- Ensure the *Mobile data* is defined **ON** (green), tapping the change to allow it if required.

- If this hasn't worked well, you might enter

configurations manually for your unique network operator. To get into these configurations, scroll right down to Mobile data network and tap on it to gain access to an option generally called *APN*.

- You could additionally have the ability to re-download the configurations from your Sim card by scrolling to the low area of the APN configurations website and tap reset configurations.

- If none of the strategies gets you connected to a mobile data network, I would suggest contacting your mobile network issuer for additional help, as they are capacitated to sending the configurations without delay to your device from their end.

I'd suggest most effectively the utilization of Mobile internet for email messages and general web surfing. If you watch many movies or pay attention to many online pieces of music, you might use your computer data bundle very quickly and turn into getting billed extra sums in addition to your month-to-month invoice. Test with your network service provider to discover your computer data charge, and look at the telephone bill app to know your recent data for each month.

Enabling and Disabling the iPhone Internet Connection

How to Turn OFF your Wireless Connection

If your wireless connection is slow, you may want to turn it off for a short time to let you use mobile data as a substitute - be aware of lots of information you are probable to apply! Apple has made it very quick and smooth to do this.

Open Control Centre by swiping up from below the Display Screen. In Control Centre you will see a row of six spherical icons which might be White when the function is turned **ON** and Gray while it's **OFF**. The Wi-Fi image must be the second icon from the left, so tap this to put it out.

As soon as you have completed that, the wireless symbol next on your network name at the top of the display will disappear, displaying you're no longer linked to the internet. In case your iPhone has a Sim card in it, the wireless image will be replaced by the data connection indicator (4G, 3G, E, GPRS) and you will be back again on Mobile Network. Just do not forget to turn your Wireless ON back to keep away from those pesky data charges!

How to Turn OFF Mobile Data

Your mobile data connection can be turned off in much the same way as Wi-Fi, but as it's not such a standard requirement, the setting to do so is buried a little deeper in the handset menus.

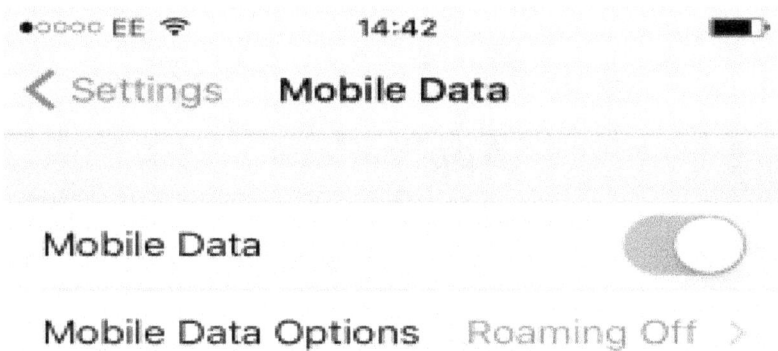

●○○○○ EE 📶   14:42   ▬▬▷

❮ Settings   **Mobile Data**

Mobile Data   ⬭

Mobile Data Options   Roaming Off ❯

1.   From the Home screen, locate and tap on Settings.

2.   In the top section of the main settings menu, select on Mobile or Cellular (you would see one word or the other, depending on your mobile network).

3.   At the top of the Mobile Data menu, there is a switch for Mobile Data. When enabled, the switch shows green. To turn off your data connection, tap the change. With your data connection turned off, your phone will only access the internet if you connect to a Wi-Fi network.

How To Use App Store To Find Applications

Do you want to download apps to your iPhone? With such a lot to choose from in the app store, it's hard to realize where to begin! Right here's the way to get the tasty morsels of application from the Apple application store for your iPhone.

How to Download New App on iPhone

Downloading new applications via the app store is a reasonably direct process; however, when you download your first app, you can have a bit of set up to do in regards to your **Apple ID**. Comply with the instructions underneath, and you will have your iPhone ever downloading apps right away!

- To begin, tap the App Store icon at the home screen of your new iPhone.

- The store will open up with the Featured Apps web page. This may display to you the applications presently being promoted, either by Apple themselves or via the App developers. You can scroll down the page to look at distinct sections, and each areas' icons can be swiped through to examine which apps are being featured.

- Tapping **See All** at the right-hand side of every featured segment will show you that option in more detail.

- At the top left of the first website, you could select on **Categories**, which breaks up the App Store into broadly titled segments, without difficulty navigating through the sections. Tap **Cancel** at the top to return to the presented apps web page.

- In the categories, you may see sub-categories to make it simpler to browse the kind of apps you're looking for.

- At the bottom of the leading web page, you'll find links to various sections of the App Store. Featured you will see, and top Charts which are self-explanatory - brief access to **"Top 40 applications"** style lists of free and paid applications if you want to scroll through.

Explore allows you to look for what human nearby are downloading, which can be quite useful when trying to find your way around a new location, or in case you're at a sporting or musical occasion.

Tapping **SEARCH** at the lower part of the display screen allows you to enter the name of an App you have heard about or recommended to you.

Updates, as the name implies, is where you can control your apps and download updates.

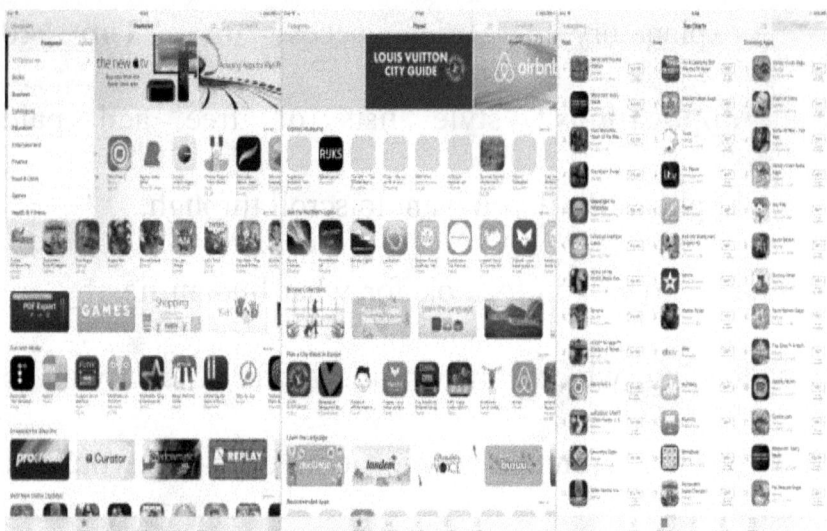

- When using the search function, anything you type into the field causes results to auto-fill on the web page. Tap the Search suggestion you like, to see what apps it brings up.

- If the button to the right-hand side of the app's name says **Download**, the app is free, and there will be no price to yourself. Tapping the word **Download** will change the box to say **Install**.

- Tapping Install will start the download process. If

there is a fee, the price would be displayed in place of the term **Download**, and you'll be asked to link a card to your **Apple ID** to pay for this and any future purchases.

- If that is the first app you have attempted to download on your new iPhone, you may be requested to input your **Apple ID** information. If you have already got an **Apple ID** (if this is your first iPhone you will be prompted to create one at some stage in the initial set up process), you can tap use existing **Apple ID**, and **Sign in**. In case you do not have an Apple ID, select create new Apple ID and observe the on-screen instructions to create your free Apple ID account. When you have already introduced your Apple ID by signing into iCloud, you will need to put in your password.

- For ease of use, you may set a time hold of 15 or

more minutes before your password is needed again. This can make it smooth to install several apps in one session as you may not need to enter your password every time. Tap to regularly require your security password or require after 15 minutes, as you deem fit to you.

- You'll necessarily need to accept the iTunes Terms & Conditions, and the Apple privacy policy (which you can get dispatched to yourself via email by tapping the supplied hyperlink) by tapping **Agree**, then show that you genuinely do agree by tapping **Agree** again!

- With your account signed in and the agreements handled, your app can now be downloaded. Tap ok for this to happen.

- When the application is downloading, you'll see a blue development indicator in the shape of a circle, with a square at the middle. Tap this if you want to pause/restart the download for any cause.

- When the application has been successfully installed, the progress button changes to an open button to which will let you access the app. When installing, the app will also appear in the first available home display area. However, you can without difficulty move this in case you want!

While you've completed your task in the store, press the **Home button** at the bottom of the iPhone's front panel to return to your home display screen. Swipe across to see your newly installed apps!

How to Manage Apps on iPhone
How to re-arrange iPhone Apps

Whenever you download a brand-new app, it is automatically going to primarily occupy the next available space on your home display. You can easily re-arrange the applications into any order you want. To try this, tap and hold your finger on the application icon for some seconds. All the icons start jiggling. Now, all you want to do is place your finger on the image you need to move and drag it to the precise position of your choice. You can walk in between the display screen by moving the icon at the edge of the screen for a 2nd or 3rd. When you have finished, press the home button to go back to the standard display.

How to Organize iPhone Folders

Setting your apps in folders makes it loads quickly to search out the app you're searching. In preference to scrolling through pages of apps, you could click on the appropriate folder and go immediately to the app you want.

To create a folder, all you need to do is place your finger on an app icon until it starts to jiggle similarly to when you are re-arranging apps. Then pull and drop an application icon at the top of another app icon. This will place both applications in a folder. You may change the name of the folder and move in a few more apps if you need. If you have completed the process, press the home button.

To move objects out of a folder, open up the folder first then maintain your finger on one of the application icons in it until they jiggle, then tap and hold on your selected app, and drag it out of the folder to the home screen. If you pull the remaining last app out of the folder, the folder itself will vanish.

How to Delete iPhone Apps

When you have downloaded an application which you do not like or that you don't need again, you may delete it off your iPhone. To do that, just press and keep your finger on the app icon till the icons begin jiggling about. You ought to then see an x at the top left corner of every icon. Tap the **"x"** to dispose of the app. Do not worry; you cannot take away inbuilt apps on phone or contacts by doing this so that it won't cause any problem.

CHAPTER 4

Sending Emails & Attachments from iPhone

To send an email, you ought to have already created an email account on your iPhone.

- Find and open the app on your home display screen. This looks like a White Envelope, and if you've acquired emails already, there may be a pink badge on it which represents some unread email messages.

- The email App will open up your brand-new E-mail. To view your inbox, Tap **INBOX or ALL INBOXES** at the top left-hand nook of the screen.

- When you can see your E-mail inbox, select the **COMPOSE BUTTON**. This looks like a pen and paper, and it's located at the top-right nook of the email inbox screen.

- The screen will now show blank email, ready to begin writing.

- New emails will regularly send from your default electronic mail account (which is usually the first one you have added). When you have multiple accounts on your iPhone and want to switch the accounts to send from, it is easy to do. Touch the **CC/BCC, FROM** collection which shows the e-mail address with which you're sending from, then Touch the e-mail address shown to change it to another account.

- To add a **recipient**, Tap into the **TO** field. To browse your contact list, Tap the + button at the right-hand aspect of the display. You could additionally start to type their name, and any matching contacts would be shown allowing you to pick the one you are searching out for. In case you don't have the Tap saved for your device already, simply Tap the **TO** Field and start typing the E-mail address you wish to send to.

- Utilize the **SUBJECT** box to add a title to your e-mail.

- Tap into the main window (above the pre-loaded send from my iPhone signature) to put the cursor there and type your message. When you're ready to send your e-mail, select **Send** at the top right-hand nook.

How to Add an Attachment to E-Mail

iPhones can feature photos and videos from the device as an attachment ever since iOS 7 was launched in 2013. However, you can now additionally add attachments from online storage including Google Drive or Dropbox, especially with the recent **iOS 13, iOS 12 and iOS versions** to come.

How to Attach an Image or Video From Your iPhone

- Begin by creating and accessing your email account as stated above.

- To feature/attach a picture or video, Tap the **CAMERA** icon to the right of the keyboard's top level.

- Please navigate through the image folders you've created for your iPhone to discover the image or video you want to transfer and Tap it to choose it.

- To choose the image or video and connect it for your email, Tap **USE**. You can attach one at a time. However, nothing is stopping you from adding any other one!

- Provided that you've launched your internet connection, Tap **SEND** to get it sent immediately.

How to Add a Document From an Online Storage App

To add accessories from a web storage account such as **Dropbox or Google Drive**, you'll need to have the App for that service installed on your iPhone and be signed directly into your account in the App to gain access to your documents.

- Create your email as described above, then select the paper clip icon to the right of the keyboard's top line.

- By default, your **iCloud Drive Storage** will open. If that is where your file is, navigate through your folders and choose it. To import an item from external storage, Tap **SOURCE**.

- The first time you use this feature, you'll want to

allow access to which you will use an option storage space source. Tap **More**.

- The manage location display allows you to select the storage Apps you want to include documents from elsewhere. Tap the switch to the right of your preferred App to allow/enable it (it turns green) then Tap **DONE**.

- You'll then be back at the **iCloud Drive Screen**. Tap Source once more to open up your storage choices.

- This time all the storage space Apps you enabled in the previous display screen should be accessible for you in the menu. Tap the Appropriate one to discover the files and folders therein.

- Please navigate through the folders to locate the file you are considering, and Tap it to attach it to your email.

- When you've attached your document(s), Tap **SEND** to get document attached and sent to your contact(s)!

How To Proceed Whenever Your iPhone Email Does not Work

Among the predominant benefits of the iPhone is it will keep you connected to almost anybody from anywhere. Whether it's by text, social press, or e-mail, your iPhone is your marketing communications lifeline to the world. That is one of the things that makes it so irritating whenever your e-mail is no longer working (it's so annoying if you would like to get an electronic email for your business or job).

You'll find so many issues that could affect your iPhone form downloading e-mail, which explains why this section is entirely for you if you're confronted with email challenges.

You will find eight predominant steps you might use to try and solve the majority of the challenges you might be facing with e-mail.

We shall start highlighting them individually.

- **Check Your Network Connection**

Your iPhone cannot get an e-mail if it's not linked to the internet. It's essential to get access to a mobile network through your phone or a Wi-Fi network that may grant you access to e-mail.

You need to additionally ensure that Airplane mode is not enabled on your iPhone because that could quickly block contacts to mobile and Wi-Fi networks.

- **Restart Your Email App**

One quick way to repair any application not operating as anticipated is to exit and re-launch the application. That is another simple method of solving mail difficulties. To try out this method, follow the next steps:

1. Double select your iPhone Home button.

2. When the multi-tasking view shows up, find Mail.

3. Swipe Email up and close the display.

4. Click once on the Home button.

5. Tap the Mail application to re-launch it.

- **Restart Your iPhone**

If regardless your web connection is intact and you've restarted the email app, and you also see that the problem persists, the next step is one of the most typical in every **iPhone-troubleshooting guide** which is to restart your smartphone.

Sometimes it's hard for individuals to trust because we always expect that organic approach must be employed to solving problems; however, in most instances, a simple method usually is our best bet. So; restarting an iPhone can get rid of loads of issues. Sometimes your mobile phone needs a new start-up.

- **Upgrade Your iPhone iOS version**

Among the top method of troubleshooting is to ensure you have the latest version of the iOS working on your device. Updated version of the iOS fixes bugs in today's version on your phone automatically and update its functions. Practically, the problems with your e-mail is a harmful bug program which can best be set with the latest iOS upgrade or your e-mail provider has made a few changes to their configurations, and it's only the latest iOS version to guide you to cope with the change.

- **Delete, and Set-up E-mail Accounts Again**

If none of the steps enumerated above solved the issue, there might not be anything wrong with your iPhone. On the other hand, the problem can also be from the configurations used to try reference to your Email accounts. Perhaps; if you enter a wrong server address, username, or security password when establishing the accounts on your iPhone, you might not be capable of getting an Email.

If this is the case, you can begin once more by deleting the e-mail accounts from your mobile phone following a few steps below:

1. Head to Settings.

2. Go directly to the Tabs where you see Email, Contacts, and Calendar.

3.   Go through the accounts with the problem.

4.   Delete the Accounts.

5.   Delete from My iPhone in the pop-up menu in the bottom of the screen.

Having deleted the e-mail accounts, check all the settings that you can use to gain access to this accounts and feel the procedure of adding an e-mail account in your iPhone again (you might synchronize the reports to your phone through iTunes).

There are many other ways of deleting an email account from an iPhone; this and many other important information would be explained explicitly in a later edition of this book.

- **Contact Email Provider**

As of this juncture, it's time to get some excellent direct technical support for your e-mail issues.

An excellent approach is to check with your e-mail provider, such as (Google for Gmail, Yahoo, and many more.). Each Email service provider has specific ways to provide support; however, a great strategy is to log into your email accounts on the internet through a pc and then navigate to your company support link.

- **Make an Apple Store Appointment**

In case your email provider can't help, you might have a problem that is complex than you are designed for. If so, it is the best shot that you should take your iPhone-and all the info about the e-mail account-to the nearest Apple Store for tech support team (you could additionally call Apple for support). Apple stores are usually occupied, so be sure to make a scheduled appointment before moving out to avoid waiting around all day long at their offices.

- **Check Your IT Department**

If regardless you're trying to check a work Email accounts, and if the first five steps didn't work, it is most possible that the problem doesn't tally with your iPhone whatsoever. The problem may be from the email server you want to download email from. When there is a brief concern with that server or a construction change that you aren't aware, that could impact and stop your iPhone from being able to access it. So if the e-mail account is from your workplace, I'll recommend you contact and talk with the IT division for a solution.

How to Secure iPhone with Lock Screen

On an iPhone, you have a preference among a Custom Alphanumeric Code (that is a password with the use of letters and numbers), a Custom Numeric Code (figures only, however as many digits as you prefer!) or a 4-Digit Numeric Code (a fantastic old style pin!). You will need to decide which you need to use, so it is worth considering that earlier than you dive into the settings.

- Tap on the configuration icon, then scroll down and Tap on *Touch ID & Password*.

- In the **Touch ID** & Password menu, tap the blue hyperlink to turn Password ON.

- The default Security password placing is a Custom Alphanumeric Code - a complex password containing letters and digits. You could alternate this by tapping Password options.

- Tap your chosen password option to select it.

- Enter your **PASSWORD**. While you type in your secret four-digit, the display screen will increase automatically.

- Re-input your Security password to verify it. If the entered Passwords do not match, you might be returned to the first Security password access display to start over. If the Password that has been entered matches, then you will go back to the Security password menu.

- The final element to decide is how fast you want to enter your Password, which is often a balance between usability and safety. To change this setting, Tap **Require Password**.

- Pick your time out from the listing on screen by tapping the interval you want to set. A tick will appear on that line, and when you're happy with the setting, tap Back at the very top left-hand nook.

You can allow access to certain functions of your iPhone when the screen is locked. There are switches to enable the usage of *NOTIFICATIONS, SIRI*, and other components of the working gadget. Tap any of these to permit them (when **ON**, the switches can look green).

How to Set Up Touch ID to Unlock Your iPhone

Now that you have set up a Password, you may want to enable **Touch ID**, which is fingerprint recognition to unlock your Devices (meaning you might not need to type in that password, even though you could if you want to!).

Follow the instructions below to achieve this effortlessly;

- To begin setting up **Touch ID**, you will want to be within the Settings **Menu**.

- In the predominant settings menu, select **Touch ID & Password.**

- Input your **Password** to access the settings.

- Tap **Add a Fingerprint**.

- To start including your fingerprint, place your finger or thumb onto the *Home button*, however, do not press it. Lift and replace your finger as instructed on-screen, shifting it very slightly as you achieve this. When the center of your fingerprint has been scanned, you'll be requested to place your finger in unique positions on the home button to experiment the edges.

- While your fingerprint is fully scanned, you will see the whole screen, displaying that your print has been captured and Touch ID is ready. Touch **Continue**.

- As you add fingerprints, they'll be numbered. You can change the names (so you recognize which print is which) or delete fingerprints from the phone by Tapping the name after which editing or deleting as required.

- When you've modified the name of fingerprint, Tap **Done** on the keyboard to keep the new name.

- **TOUCH ID** will be without delay activated for unlocking your iPhone, and for **Apple Pay**. To enable iTunes and App Store Purchases to be authorized alongside with your fingerprint, Tap the switch to carefully turn it **ON,** then get into your Apple ID password.

You can upload as much as five Fingerprints, so putting in place fingerprint access for your family members may be carried out too. A phrase of warning though; remember that in case you've introduced the capacity to use fingerprint scanning to authorize iTunes and App Store buys, anybody who's fingerprint is added can do this too!

CHAPTER 5

Undisclosed iPhone Camera Features

Do you want to make the full use of your iPhone camera when you take photographs? As it's easy to take a photo with your iPhone, the excellent and crucial iPhone digital camera features are hidden from regular iPhone users. So; in this section, you'll find out the seven concealed iPhone camera features that every iPhone users must use.

- Swipe Left for Swift Access to Your iPhone Camera. How often have you seen or witness an incredible scene in front of your eyes, only to discover that it's gone at the time you're prepared to take a photo? You can improve your possibilities of taking a perfect shot if you know how to use your camera effectively.

- In case your iPhone is locked, you can press the

home button to wake up your phone, and then swipe left through the lock display.

- The camera will open immediately, and you won't even need to enter your password to unlock your iPhone. This trick will make you begin capturing in less than a second!

- However, what if you're already making use of the iPhone, and also you want to quickly access the digital camera, swipe up from the lower part of the screen to open the Control Center as shown below.

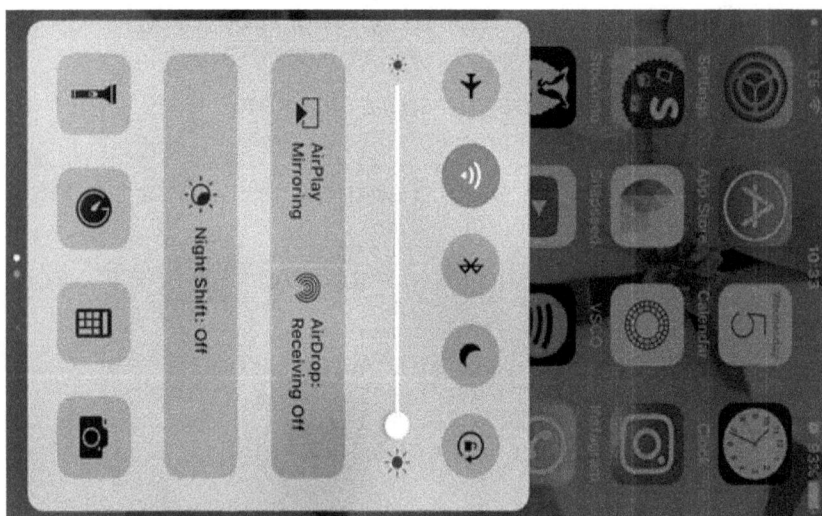

From here, select the camera icon in the bottom right, and you're ready to start taking pictures!

How to Set Focus and Exposure

If you haven't set focus and exposure, the iPhone can do it for you automatically. Usually, it can be a reasonably good job. Furthermore, that's how most iPhone users take almost all their photographs.

There are a few times, though, when autofocus fails - or when you wish to Focus on something in addition to the apparent subject.

That's when you'll want to create focus manually. That is super easy to do - Tap the location on the display where you'd prefer to set Focus, and the camera deals with others.

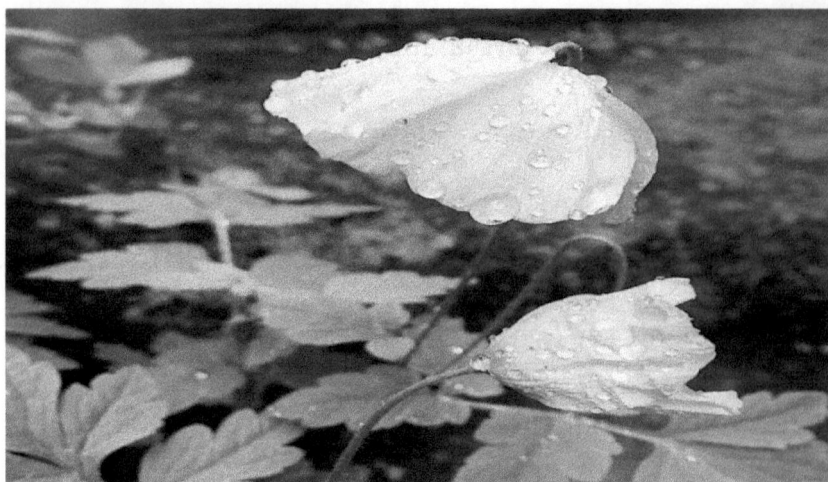

What distinction does focus make? If you go through the picture above, the Focus is defined on the blossom in the foreground. The topic is bright and shiny, as the bloom petals and leaves in the backdrop are blurred.

When you Tap on the screen to set Focus, the camera automatically sets the exposure. The exposure refers to improving the brightness of an image. So it's essential to get the exposure right if you are taking your picture.

NB: *When you wish to set **Focus**, check out the display to find out if the lighting of the image appears suitable. If it seems too vibrant or too darkish, you can change exposure before taking the picture.*

After you've Tapped on the screen to create focus and exposure, the exposure slider with a sun icon will be observed. Swipe up to help make the picture brighter or right down to make the image darker.

Efficaciously setting focus and exposure is one of the primary element skills that a photographer must master. When it takes merely a few Taps to modify focus and exposure, it's essential that you do it effectively to Focus on the most crucial components of the complete picture.

The task is that every photograph takes a specific method of focus and exposure setting.

Things that work notably for landscapes don't work

almost as properly for night or tour photos.

How to Lock Focus and Exposure with AE/AF Lock

The iPhone also allows you to lock each one of the appealing points; focus and exposure. So why would you need to lock those functions while going for a picture?

- The principle motive is if anything changes in the scene, including a moving subject or altered lighting, your focus and exposure will stay unchanged.

- That's why it's a great idea to lock Focus and exposure when you're expecting motion within the picture. For instance, *Focus and exposure* lock could be beneficial in street picture taking.

- You might frame the shot, and set the focus and

exposure earlier, then obviously watch out for a person to pass-by before taking your photo.

- Once you've locked the focus and exposure, you might take several pictures of the same picture and never have to set focus and exposure each time you want to consider photos. To unlock Focus and exposure, select anywhere on the screen.

- To lock focus and exposure, Tap and retain your hands on the display screen for mere multiple seconds at the stage where you want to create the center point. A yellowish package with AE/AF lock can look near the top of the display.

Note: You can nevertheless swipe up or down on display to regulate exposure manually.

Now regardless of what happens within the framework or how you fling the iPhone, the Focus and Exposure will still be unchanged.

How to Take HDR Photos

HDR, which means *High Active Range*, is another incredible pictures tool that's included in the camera of your iPhone.

HDR picture taking with the iPhone combines three unique exposures of precisely the same image to produce one nicely exposed picture.

It's exquisite for high comparison moments with shiny and darkish areas since it allows you to fully capture extra component in both shadows and the highlights.

Some small adjustments within an editing application such as Snapseed can indeed draw out the colours and detail that were captured in the **HDR photograph**, although it still comes with fantastic well-balanced exposure.

- You'll find the HDR setting at the left side of the camera app. Tapping on HDR provides you with three options: Motion, ON, or OFF.

- Notably, it's high-quality to use HDR for panorama or landscape pictures and scenes where the sky occupies a significant area of the photograph. This enables the taking of extra fine detail in both brighter sky and the darker foreground.

- There are a few downsides to HDR, especially in conditions of pictures of motion. Because HDR is a variety of three sequentially captured photos, you might encounter "ghosts" if the picture is changing quickly. HDR images also require a long period to capture, which means that your hands may shake even while the shutter is open up.

- It's additionally essential to state that non-HDR

pictures will sometimes look much better than HDR ones, that's the reason it's a good idea to save lots of each variation of the picture. To make sure that each variant is stored, go to configurations > photos & camera, and ensure Save Normal Picture is **ON** in the *HDR section*.

- It's also well worth mentioning that the default iPhone camera application comes with an alternatively subtle *HDR impact*. A sophisticated camera application that can create much more powerful HDR results and provide you with complete control over the catch.

How to Take Snapshot in Burst Mode

- Burst mode is one of the very most useful capturing features in the iPhone's camera app. It enables you to take ten images in only one second, which makes it easy to fully capture the suitable movement shot with reduced blur.

- If you wish to activate burst setting, keep down the shutter button for half a second or longer, and the iPhone begins capturing one after another. When you've shot a burst of snap photos, after that, you can choose the lovely images from the Set and delete others.

- Burst setting is worth using each time there's any

movement or unpredictability in the

picture.

Remember utilizing it when photographing kids, animals,

birds, and splashing water.

It's also excellent for taking pictures on magical

occasions in street picture taking. Likewise, try the

utilization of burst setting to capture the correct stride or

present.

How to Take Pictures with Volume Buttons

Perhaps you have ever overlooked or missed the iPhone's tiny on-display shutter button? If so, change to the utilization of volume control keys beside your iPhone! Either of these buttons can be utilized for shutter release, and the tactile opinions you get from pressing this button is a great deal more pleasurable than pressing an electronic switch.

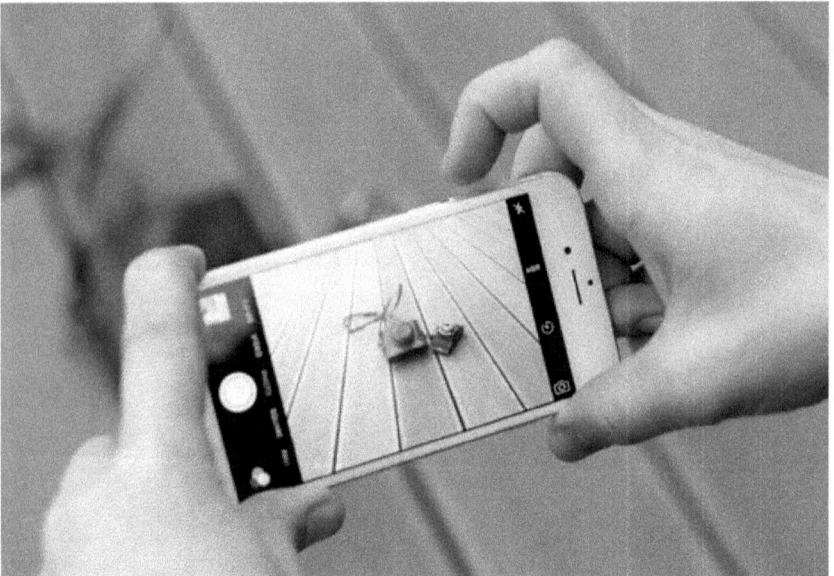

Additionally, this enables you to carry the iPhone with two hands, just as you'd grab a typical digital camera.

The only drawback of the approach is that you'll require pressing the Volume button pretty hard, which might produce camera shake. That's especially essential in low-mild or less lighted environment, where any movement of your iPhone will lead to the blurry picture.

How to Take Photographs with your Apple Headphones

Remember those white apple headphones that were included with your iPhone on purchase can be utilized for photo taking. This additionally has *Volume buttons*, and you may use these control keys to consider photos!

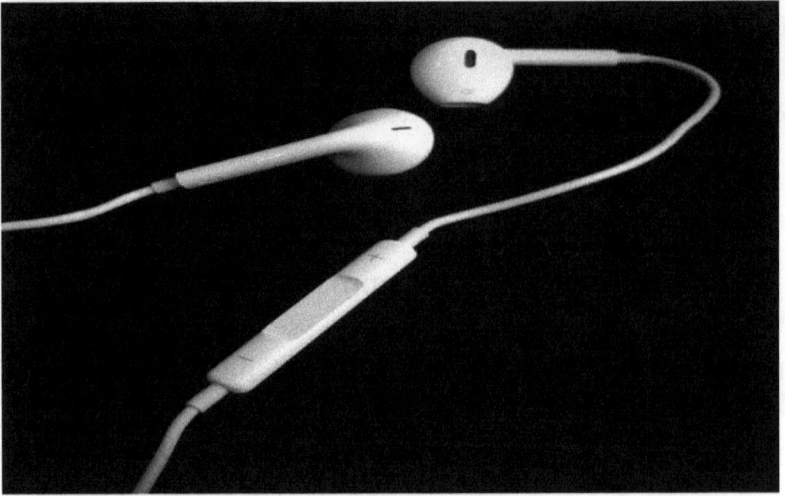

This feature is tremendously useful when you need to take discreet pictures of people you don't recognize or know in person, as you could pretend to be paying focused attention to music or making a call while you're taking pictures.

This method additionally is available when your iPhone is on a tripod. As you release the shutter with your headphones, you can get rid of any unintentional digital camera movement, which is quite essential for night time pictures, long exposure images, etc.

CHAPTER 6

How To Snap a Perfect iPhone Picture

Hipstamatic is an elegant iPhone camera application for growing unique photos with a retro or vintage appearance. It comes with an outstanding selection of analog film, zoom lens, and flash results which enable you to easily change an ordinary picture into something exceedingly thrilling, stunning or dramatic. Besides, it comes with an accessible improving and editing Set for fine-tuning your photographs in post-processing. With this section, you'll learn the step-by-step instructions when planning on taking pictures and editing and enhancing lovely images using the Hipstamatic app.

Hipstamatic Zoom lens & Film Combos

Hipstamatic is most beneficially known because of its potential to make a vast selection of retro-styled pictures based on numerous filters. The filter systems are applied when you take the photo; nevertheless, you can always change the ultimate result by just selecting different filter systems once you've used the shot.

The Hipstamatic filters get into three categories that are: zoom lens type, film type, and flash type. Before you proceed with going for a picture in Hipstamatic, you should select which zoom lens, film, and flash you want to use.

The lens decides the colours and tones in your photo. The film determines the framework or vignette across the advantage of the image (and occasionally also changes the colours of the image). The flash helps in creating distinctive lights.

The lens, film, and flash mixtures in Hipstamatic are known as "*combos.*" Through the utilization of diverse combinations of the zoom lens, film, and flash, you can create an enormous variety of image styles - from faded superior results to high comparison dark and white picture.

To give an example of how Hipstamatic can change an ordinary picture into something a lot more aesthetically attractive, check the photographs below. The first picture is the original photo without Hipstamatic filter systems applied:

Subsequent are a few examples of the same scene captured with the use of specific Hipstamatic lens and film combos:

When taking a picture with Hipstamatic, you can either permit the app to select a combo for you or try different mixtures of your desire until you locate an impact you like.

Hipstamatic includes a core set of lens, film and flash options, and many more can be found as in-app purchases.

Selecting A Camera Interface

Hipstamatic has two different camera settings/interfaces included in the application. You may use the vintage camera user interface that mimics the appearance and feel of vintage film cameras:

You can likewise utilize the *Pro camera interface,* which has a modern and professional feel. This camera mode is excellent if you want a bit of manual control while taking pictures:

If you wish to select from both camera settings, Tap both opposing arrows icon (arrows are either facing each other or aside depending on which digital camera setting you are employing).

How to Take Pictures with Hipstamatic Vintage Camera

You are going to learn how to consider pictures using the vintage camera mode in Hipstamatic. Be sure you've chosen the primary camera interface. If you're presently in the pro camera setting, select the opposing arrows to change to a traditional setting.

When working with Classic mode, you can change between your front and back views of the camera by Tapping the flip icon (curved arrow) in the bottom right of the screen.

How to Take a Picture with Basic Camera

- When you point the camera at a picture, you'll view it in the *sq. Viewfinder*. When capturing, you can choose from viewfinder alternatives.

- You can both view the picture with no filter systems (lenses, movies, etc.) applied, alternatively, you can see in real-time, what the actual photograph can look like following when the shot has been taken using your chosen filters (you'll understand how to select lens, movies, etc. later as you read further).

- To change between those two viewfinder options, Tap the small dark switch in the bottom right of the viewfinder (as shown below):

When the switch is at the **OFF** function (completely black colour), you won't start to see the picture with all of your selected filters applied, but, when the photograph is used, the filters will be employed to the image.

When the switch is within the ON position (yellow eyeball icon will be shown).

I endorse getting the viewfinder change in the ON position, and that means you can easily see the impact of the existing zoom lens, film, and flash combo.

When you've composed your shot, take the picture by Tapping the yellow shutter button at the very top right.

NB: You can additionally enlarge the viewfinder by double-Tapping the viewfinder windows. You'll be able to select the viewer once to consider the shot.

If you wish to start to see the picture you've taken, Tap the square image thumbnail icon in the bottom still left of the screen. The image gallery can look displaying a preview of the photos you've shot with Hipstamatic, as shown below.

If you wish to see a much larger model of a specific

photo, select the picture you want to see. When viewing the entire sized image, you'll see which film/zoom lens/flash combo used, as well as the location where the image was taken.

How to Decide on a Zoom lens/Film/Flash Combo

- For you to specify the appearance and design of your picture, you'll need to pick from the several options of lens and film (and flash if preferred).

- You can either decide on a preset combo from the favourites screen, or you create your combo from scrape. Taking into consideration the preset combo, first of all, begin by Tapping the circular icon (the next from the cheapest right-hand part) as shown in the red group below:

- Swipe across to see the number of cameras with diverse zoom lens/film/flash combos, however; don't Tap on the cameras yet. Every camera comes with an example photo showing the type of picture style that unique combo will generate.

- Tap and keep a camera to see more information in what configurations to be utilized, then select the x to come back to the standard display screen.

- To select a specific combo from the favorites screen, Tap on the camera combo you want to use.

On the other hand, you can allow the app to arbitrarily shuffle the combo on every occasion you are taking picture shot, providing you with a definite effect for every chance. If you like this option, select the shuffle icon (two arrows at the top right) and pick your chosen option:

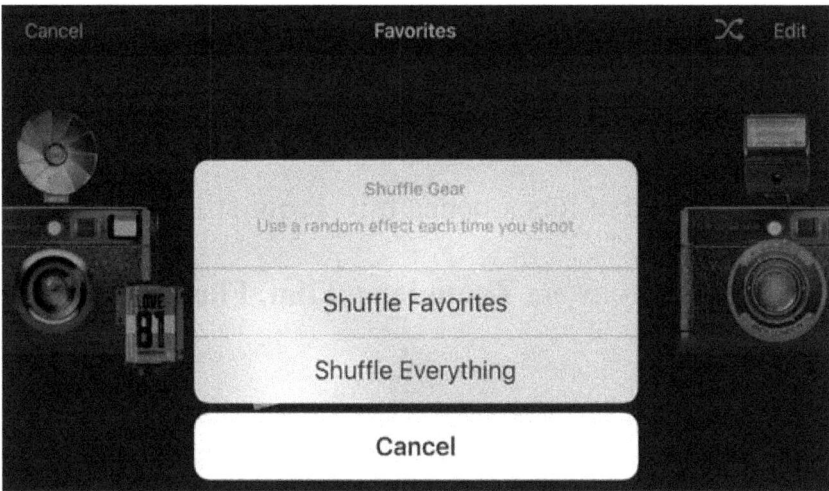

- When you've chosen a camera combo from the listed favourites, or the shuffle option, you'll be taken back to the camera to be able to begin capturing.

- You can additionally create your own

lens/film/flash combos and upload these to the report on favorites. To achieve that, Tap the spherical icon (second from right hands side) in the bottom of the screen to access the preferences display.

- Swipe over the cameras to the much right, then select the newest favourites (+) icon.

- The proceeding screen will show a preview image with three icons beneath it. From still left to right, these icons are **Zoom lens, Film, Flash.**

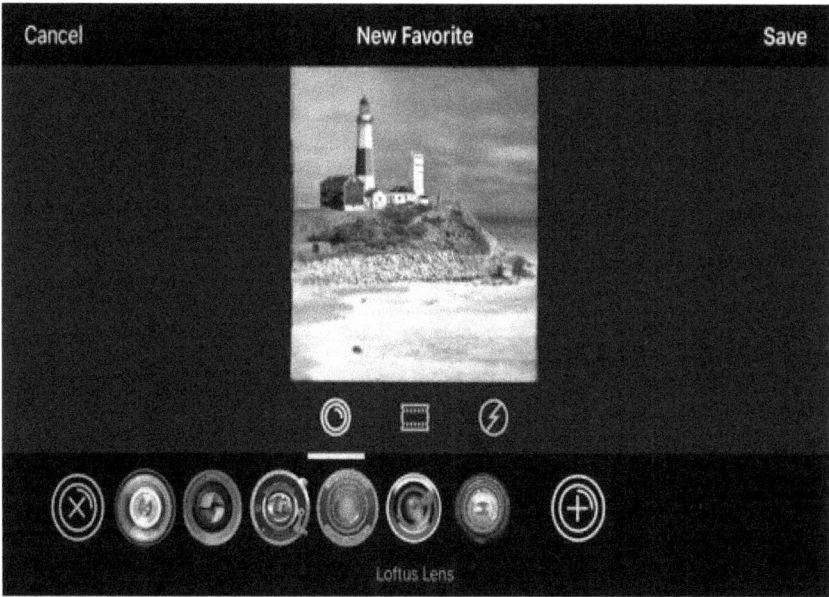

- Begin by selecting the type of zoom lens that you want to use - recollect that the zoom lens adjusts the colours and shades of your picture. When you choose the particular lens in the bottom of the screen, the preview image changes showing what impact that zoom lens could have on your picture.

- When you've chosen the lens that you like, Tap the Film icon (middle icon) under the picture preview.

The film determines the framework or vignette round the advantage of the image, and additionally, it may change the firmness. Pick the film style that you want from underneath of the display:

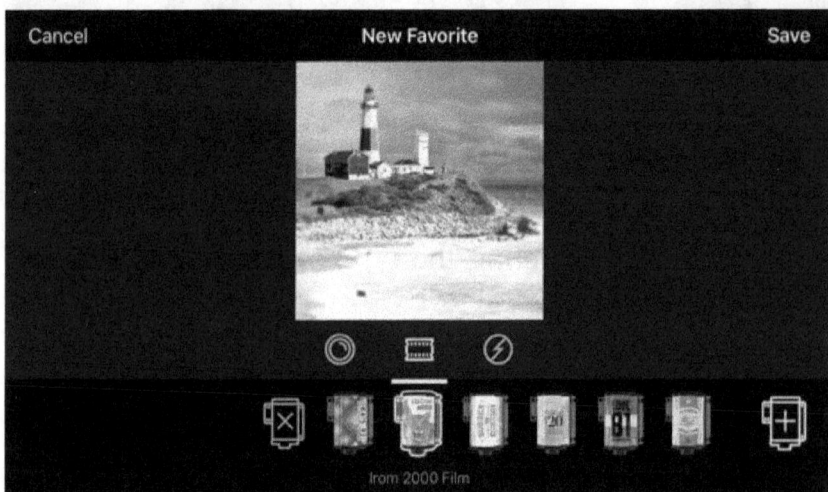

- Next, select the flash icon (right-hand icon) under the image preview. The flashes put in a particular lightning impact on your picture. If you wish to apply flash, choose your decision from underneath of the display, typically, select No Flash.

- You'll discover that there's an advantage (+) indication for the zoom lens, film and flash options - Tapping this icon goes to the Hipstamatic store where you can buy new lenses, movies, and flashes to increase your Sets.

- When you're pleased with your selected combo, Tap Save at the very top right part of the screen. On the next screen, you can enter a name for your combo, then select Done:

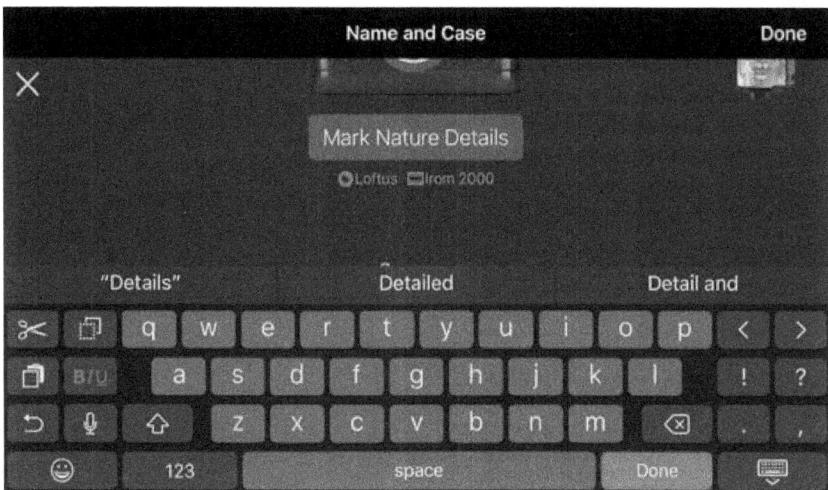

- Your newly added combo can look in the set of Favorites. To use this combo, select onto it, and also you'll be taken back to the camera and that means you can begin snapping:

- There's one other method of choosing a combo of zoom lens, film and flash for capturing. Remember, there's a back view and front side view in traditional camera setting - on the back camera view, Tap the **Turn icon** (curved arrow in the bottom right) that may change you to the leading camera view.

- To select a particular zoom lens, swipe over the large zoom lens in the centre of the display till you start to see the zoom lens you desire.

- To choose a film, select the film icon at the still left of the display screen. Swipe up or down on the rolls of the film until you find the lens you wish.

- To find out more records regarding a specific film,

as well as test pictures, Tap the move of film - select Done to exit the film information.

- When you've selected the film you want to use, Tap the camera body at the right of the screen to return to the leading camera view.

- To select away a flash, select the **Flash icon** (second from lower still left) then swipe over the distinctive flash options. If you don't want to use flash, choose the No Flash option. Tap Done to come back to the leading camera view.

- If you wish to buy more lens, movies and flashes to increase your Sets, Tap the **SHOPPING CART SOFTWARE** icon (second from bottom level right). You will see the presented products or visit a particular item. If you wish to exit the shopping cart software, Tap **Done**.

- When you're content with the zoom lens/film/flash

combo which you've selected, select the **Flip icon** (curved arrow in the bottom right) to come back to the back camera view, then start taking pictures!

How to Switch Flash ON & OFF

When you're capturing with the back camera view, you'll observe a black colour slider below the sq. Viewfinder. This will help you to select if the flash should be brought ON or not if you are going for a picture.

Whenever the flash slider reaches the center, the flash is powered down.

When the flash slider is moved left, your selected flash effect will be applied on the photo; however the flash at the front end of your iPhone won't fire on.

When the flash slider is moved to the right, your selected flash effect will be employed to the photograph, and the flash at the front end of your iPhone will fire to provide more light on your subject.

How to Change Shutter Speed

- At the very top right of the camera, the display is the **shutter velocity dial**. Modifying the shutter rate does a couple of things - it modifies the exposure of the image (how gleaming it seems) and impacts how motion is captured.

- The lower the Volume on the dial, the slower the shutter speed. A slow shutter acceleration results into a brighter image, and an effortless shutter swiftness leads into a darker picture. You might use this feature to produce artistically shiny photos or very darkish moody pictures.

- Inside a case where you're capturing a scene with moving subjects, a natural shutter rate will freeze movement and a sluggish shutter rate will capture the action as a blur.

How to Create Multiple Exposures

Hipstamatic gives you to generate thrilling dual exposure pictures. You take two different picture, and then your camera combines them. That is a fun strategy to apply and can result in some exciting artwork and abstract images.

- To begin with, creating this kind of photograph, slide the **Multiple Exposure switch** (at the top left-hand side of the camera display) left such that it turns yellowish:

- Take your first picture by Tapping the yellow shutter button at the right. You will notice that the multiple exposure switch has moved to the right such that only half of the yellow square is seen:

- Position your camera at a different subject matter or view, then take the next shot. You'll start to see the **"Multi Revealing"** message show up as the app combines both images.

- If you wish to view the two times exposure image on your gallery, select the square image thumbnail icon at the bottom left of the screen. Tap the yellow pub near the top of the gallery to come back to the camera.

- Given that you're familiar with the functions of the vintage camera user interface, let's consider the procedure of taking pictures with the *Pro camera mode*.

How to Take Pictures with Hipstamatic Pro Camera

Hipstamatic pro camera mode gives more advanced camera application that gives you more manual control when shooting pictures.

- If you're presently using the Vintage camera mode, change to the pro camera user interface by just Tapping both opposing arrows at the low area of the screen as shown below:

- The pro digital camera interface appears very distinctive to the classic interface which doesn't have any retro styling, but has a larger square viewfinder with icons around the edges:

- Let's begin the usage of those camera icons to customize the final picture. In case you're using the camera in landscape orientation, as shown above, the top-right icon allows you to change the **Aspect Ratio**:

- The Aspect ratio decides the width and height of images. Choosing the 1:1 aspect percentage will result in an excellent square image, as the 16:9 proportion will be more full than its elevation. The next icon in the red circle below gives you to choose different flash options, including *Flash On, Flash Auto,* and *Constant Light*:

The icon under the flash icon will help you to switch to the front camera to be able to have a self-portrait. While in the bottom right of the display will be the two opposing arrows that may take you back to the **Classic vintage style** camera.

The icon in the bottom left of the screen gives you to choose which zoom lens/film/flash combo you should employ - similar from what you did with the entire classic camera mode:

After Tapping the icon, you can progressively swipe through the various combos until you locate an effect that suits your interest, or Tap the plus (+) icon to create a new combo. Tap on the combo you want to apply to return to the camera:

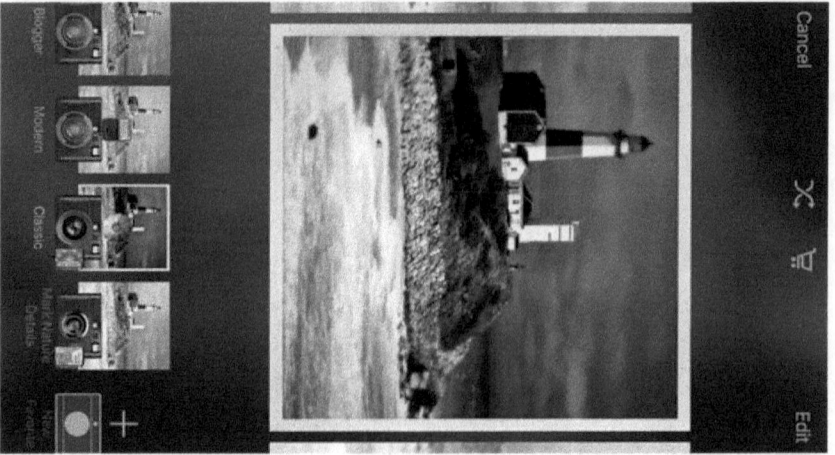

The **"M"** icon (at the right-hand side of the shutter button as shown below) stands for **Manual**, and it permits you to fine-tune the camera settings before taking your shot:

When you Tap the **Manual (m)** icon, a bar of icons will

appear in its place:

The **round target icon** allows you to adjust the focus manually. The **magnifying glass icon** helps you to zoom in. Each of these settings is modified by making use of the slider at the bottom of the display screen.

The **+/- icon** turns on the exposure slider which lets you alter the brightness up or down for brighter or darker photographs:

For the fun part! The **ISO** and **Shutter Speed** (running man icon) settings allow you to manage and control exposure and how motion appears in your photograph:

- If you wish to create motion blur when photographing an instant running subject matter, you'll need a *slow shutter velocity* and a *minimal ISO* (a minimum ISO facilitates preventing the picture from being over-exposed).

- To begin with, select the **ISO icon**, and use the slider to lessen the ISO to the lowest selection of number feasible. Then Tap the Shutter Rate icon (operating man) and move the slider to reduce the shutter rate to ensure that the picture appears almost too bright.

- The reason behind this is that; the brighter the picture, the slower the shutter acceleration, which equals higher movement blur of moving topics.

- If you're capturing in fantastic daytime conditions, you will learn that your sluggish shutter images appear too vibrant. That is why it's typically more comfortable to take at dawn or nightfall, or on darkish overcast times, to fully capture excellent show shutter photos.

- The final camera function is White Balance (lamp icon) that allows you to change the shade temperature on the scale from blue to yellow:

- The white balance enables you to warm up or keep down the colours, either to get perfect colour balance or for creative impact. You can pull the slider left to help make the colours warmer (i.e. more yellow), and move to the right to make sure they are more refreshing (i.e., extra blue):

This is undoubtedly a proper setting for indoor capturing situations where the scene is illuminated by using artificial light with a yellow coloration cast. You can merely pull the white balance slider till you're pleased with the colour firmness shown in the viewfinder:

How to Edit Pictures in Hipstamatic

Hipstamatic isn't taken into account as a professionally graded picture editor. It merely has a significant number of user-friendly improving features that will help you get the images simply perfect, such as the potential to choose a different combo such as zoom lens, film, and flash you can use when planning on taking pictures.

- To access the modifying mode, whether or not you're using the vintage camera or the pro camera, select the sq. Image thumbnail, which ultimately shows the previous picture taken:

- In the image gallery, Tap the picture you need to edit, then Tap the edit icon (3 circles) at the lowest part of the display screen as shown below:

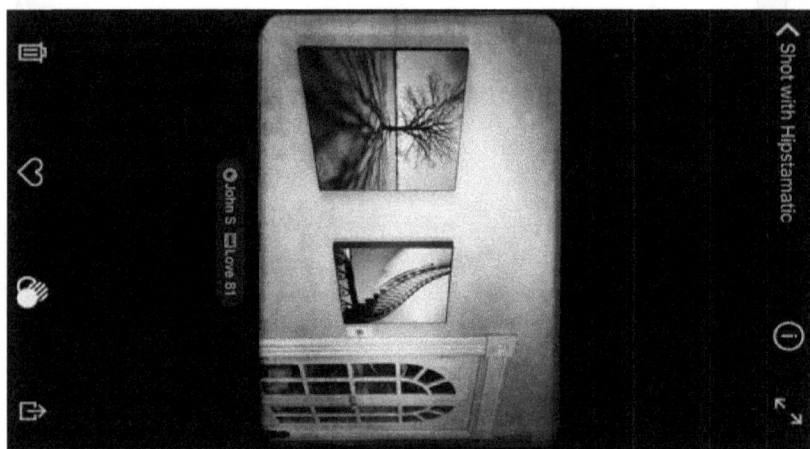

- Swipe through the preset combos in the bottom of the screen, Tapping on any that you prefer to see what impact it is wearing your image. Once you've chosen a preset that you want, use the slider to change the strength of the result till you're content with the final result. Tap **Save** when you're done editing.

- Much like the one-Tap presets, there are a few of other modifying alternatives which you can use to improve your picture. Tap the edit icon (three circles), then select the choice icon (three sliders) situated merely above the configurations icon.

- Below your image, you'll visit a row of icons which may be used to fine-tune and edit the photo.

- Conclusively; Hipstamatic gives you to create an array of picture patterns, which include retro, classic, and dark and white.

- The application has two different kinds of camera

settings (classic and pro), to be able to select to shoot using whichever interface you like. Each parameter can help you choose a zoom lens/film/flash combo, to enable you to always create the complete appearance and feel that you envisioned.

- The editing tools in the application enable you to fine-tune the picture when you've taken the shot, with the choice to decorate and improve the effect you used - or completely change the totality of the picture.

With such a great deal of unique visual combos presented within this app, you can create excellent images, indeed with an incredible artistic edge.

CHAPTER 7

How to Blend iPhone Images with Superimpose Application

The superimpose application offers a fantastic group of gear for combining two iPhone photographs into a variety of approaches. You might change the backdrop around your subject matter, put in a creative consistency overlay, or create a distinctive double exposure that mixes two photographs collectively. Superimpose additionally provides fundamental editing alternatives, including preset filters and colour and exposure adjustments. With this section, you'll locate a way to use the superimpose application to replace the backdrop in your iPhone photos and create an incredible double exposure impact.

How to Replace the Backdrop of a Graphic Image

You can replace the backdrop in virtually any iPhone picture with this process you are going to learn which works satisfactorily with photos which have a smooth structure and a solid colour contrast between your subject and the backdrop.

Follow the step-by-step instructions below meticulously.

Import Your Photos

When you open the superimpose app, you'll note there are four predominant areas as shown below that are *Home, Transform, Mask, and Filtering*. The application begins inside the home section, and that means you can import your pictures:

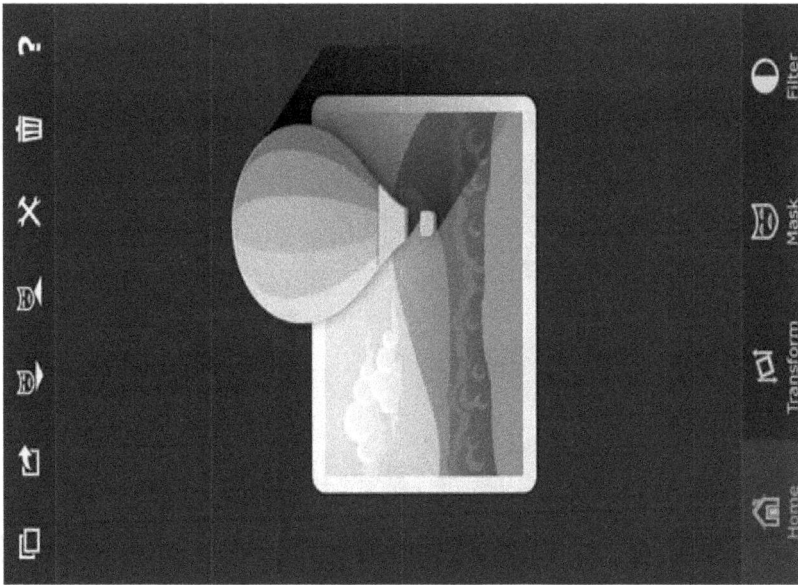

- When working on superimposes app, you will need to open both a background and a foreground picture. For the substance of changing background, the backdrop image is the picture that will become the newest background. The foreground picture is the picture with most of your subject.

- To import your snap photos, ensure you're within the home portion of superimposing, then select the import icon (can be found at the top level of the screen). A section entitled import background can look close to the very best of the screen:

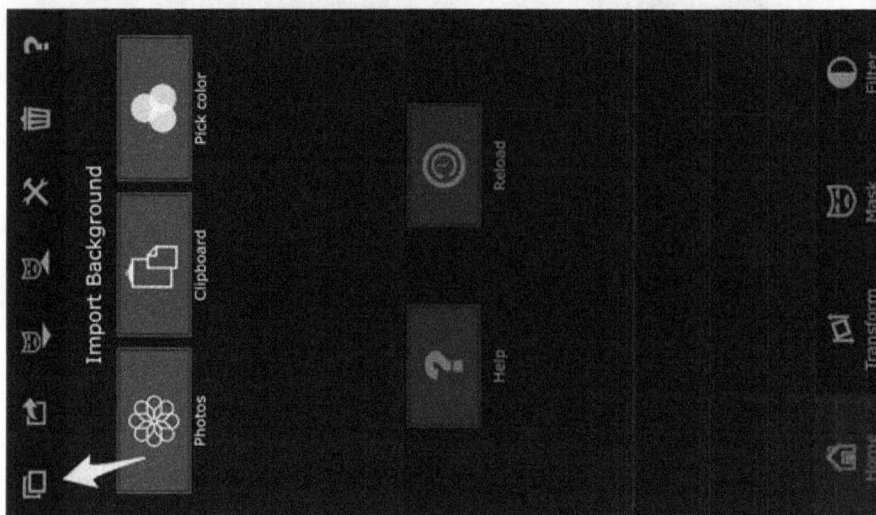

- In the import background section, Tap images to access your iPhone's picture library, then choose the photo you need to use as your background picture.

- When you insert or attach the backdrop picture, you'll see its dimensions. If you wish to exchange the dimensional level, select Constraints for growth of varied size choice or simply crop the image as you want. In case your background-size doesn't require any modification, Tap **Choose**:

- Subsequently, you will have to import your foreground photograph. Tap the import icon again (it's located at the left of the display) and also you'll see a segment titled **import foreground** near the top of the display:

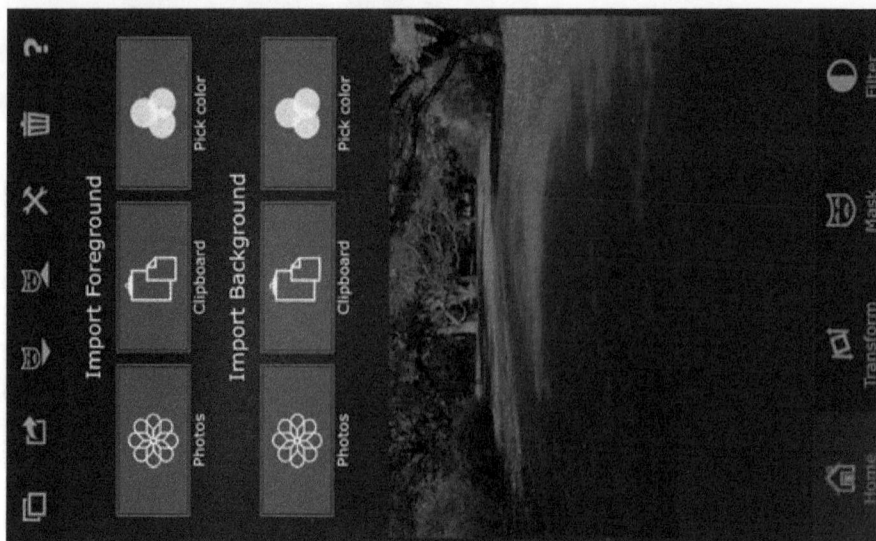

- Within the import foreground phase, Tap **Pictures**, then pick the image you wish to apply as your foreground photo.

Once more, you can crop the picture, resize it by using the **Constraints** choice, or Tap **Choose**:

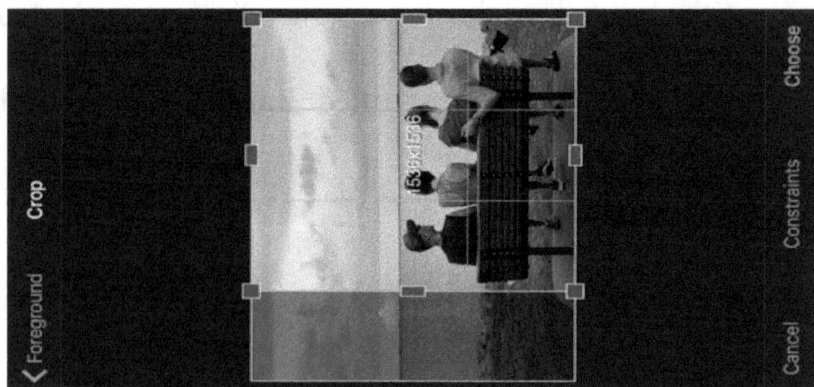

Now, you'll see that your foreground picture is superimposed over the background image:

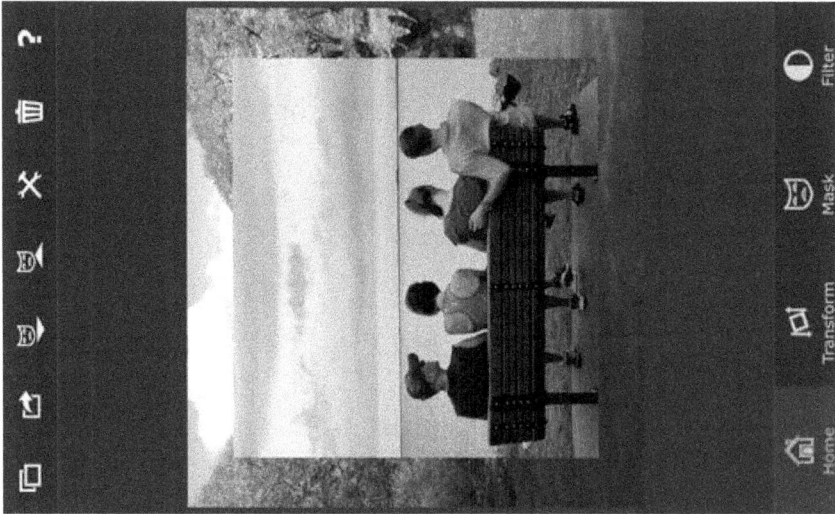

How to Reposition Foreground Image

Now you can resize and reposition the foreground image, and that means you can have it in the right position over the backdrop image. For you to now access the resizing and repositioning tools, select the Transform option at the bottom of the screen.

You'll remember that the foreground picture will have

deals on the edges (for resizing) and the sides (for rotating). If you wish to move the foreground image around, pull the image with your finger. The image may also be resized by pinching in and from the picture.

Near the top of the Transform display, you'll observe seven different icons. These are:

- **Undo**: This function is to undo your last action.

- **Redo:** This function is to redo your previous action.

- **Merge:** This function is to merge the backdrop and foreground photos collectively with the reason to weight another foreground picture at the very top. That's useful if you want to add extra layers to your image.

- **Swap:** To carefully turn the foreground picture

horizontally or vertically, besides, to change the backdrop and foreground photos.

- **Place at Middle:** This function will position the foreground image within the guts of the backdrop photo.

- **Fit to Background:** This function will level the foreground picture to the same size as the backdrop.

- **Configurations:** This function will change the transparency and blend setting, which would be needed for developing dual exposure images.

How to Produce Masks

Masking feature will enable you to edit and control the transparency of different sections of the foreground image(s).

When you make an integral part of the foreground picture transparent, the backdrop image below it'll be seen. Quite merely, masking provides you with the liberty to remove undesirable servings of the foreground images.

You can perform this by Tapping the Mask option at the lowest area of the screen, then subsequently Tap the *Magic Wand icon* close to the right hand, which is below it to get access to the masking tools:

NB: There are six simple masking tools which are

accessible (the top six tools are displayed in the pop-up

menu, as shown below):

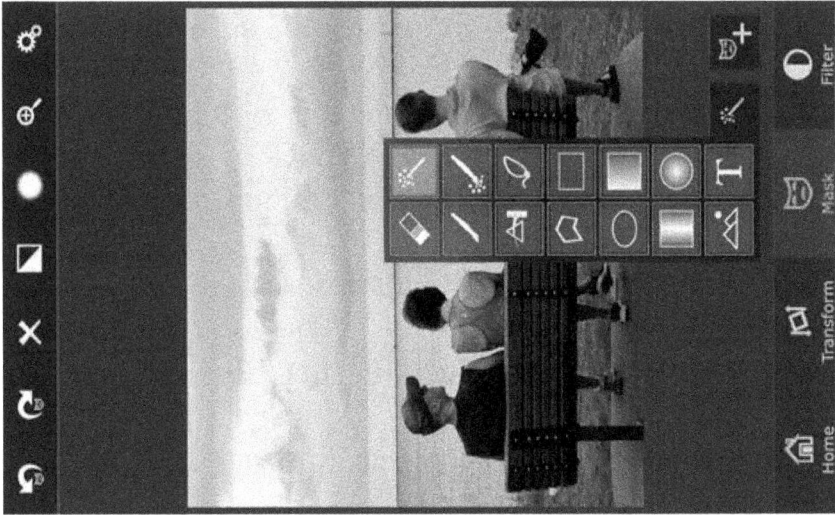

Below is a brief explanation of the six masking tools:

- **Eraser:** This tool will erase any errors you've

  manufactured in masking.

- **Magic Wand:** This function will mask all the

  similar colouration pixels encircling any point you

  Tap. You can drag or select to use the tool.

- **Brush:** Covers the whole area much just like a

  brush. This tool doesn't recognize sides, so it's

much useful for masking more significant regions.

- **Smart Brush:** This feature is comparable to the brush tool, but it recognizes the sides of the areas you're masking. Its function is to permit your selected exact locations and minimizes unintended or **unintentional brush strokes.**

- **Colour Range:** This function is similar to the magic wand tool, but instead of just the encompassing pixels, it selects all pixels related to the picture that fits the color of the pixel you Tap.

- **Lasso:** This feature will help you to pull a freehand lasso and mask anything in or from the lasso loop.

NB: Every one of the tools has configurations ascribed to it. When you've chosen the masking tool you want to use, Tap the configurations icon (can be found at the top right corner of the screen). The configurations for the tool can be seen close to underneath the screen, as shown below:

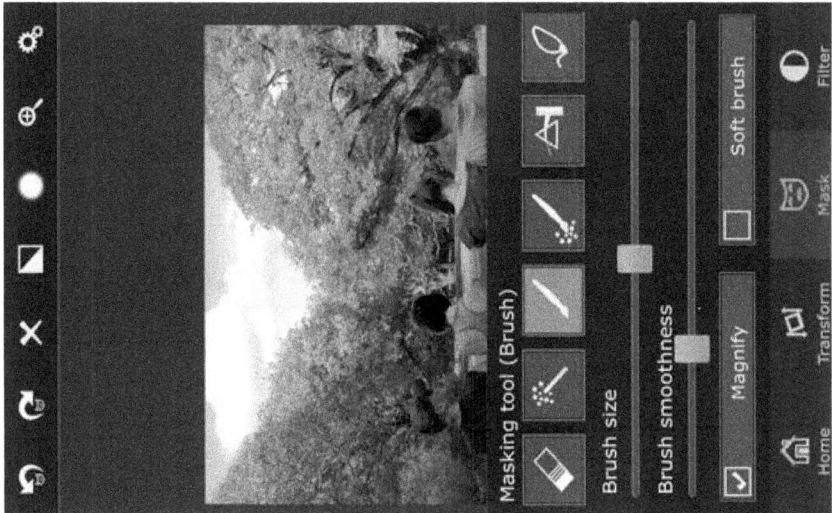

For example, you'll have the ability to regulate the **Brush**

size, Strength and Smoothness, the Threshold, and

Mask Advantage. **Threshold** determines the

effectiveness of the Mask, and Mask Advantage will help

you to choose a razor-sharp or smooth advantage.

If you wish to pick a part of the foreground image that

you need to make transparent, select or pull your finger

over the regions you want to mask. A red dot will be

shown to enable you to understand and start to see the

real place where you're focusing on:

- You'll additionally observe a pop-up. You can pinch out to focus in; to be able to get a far more in-depth view of small areas and fill up the region with an increase of accuracy. You can likewise pinch directly into zoom back to view the complete image.

- If you wish to view the areas you've masked more clearly, select the view masks icon (second icon at the very top right corner):

You will find four view masks alternatives which show exceptional coloured backgrounds, as shown below (checkerboard, red, green, or blue in colour). This depends on the colours on your foreground picture because some colored backgrounds will screen your selection flawlessly.

You can maintain focus on masking your film at the same time by using the colored masks views, or you might change to regular picture where you can view the backdrop image as you Tap the View Masks icon near the top of the display.

Save Your Valuable Masks

- After you've used the mask tools to ensure regions of your foreground image are apparent and transparent, departing merely the area of the image that you want to superimpose on the backdrop, it's a perfect concept to store your masks in the Masks library.

- This is recommended because it will help you to apply that mask on some other focus on another photo. Moreover, if you're likely to superimpose the area of the foreground picture onto every other historical photo, you'll only be asked to mask the foreground photo once.

- You might then import it onto any background picture every time you want to utilize it, which can save you from needing to mask the parts of this image every time.

- This **Mask Library** is obtainable in the home segment of the app, Tap the home option at the low area of the screen. You can select the Save Mask icon (the centre icon at the top of the screen) to save lots of the **Mask** and then Tap **Save.**

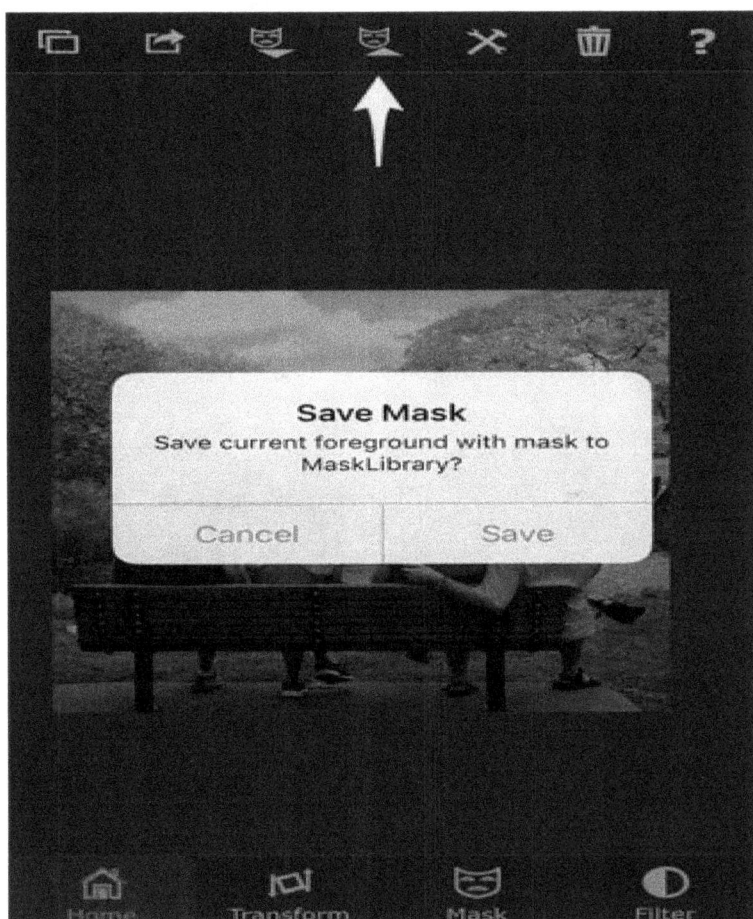

Whenever you're set to apply that masks again to a
different background photo, Tap the **Load Mask** icon
(third icon from the top left) in the **Home** section of the
app:

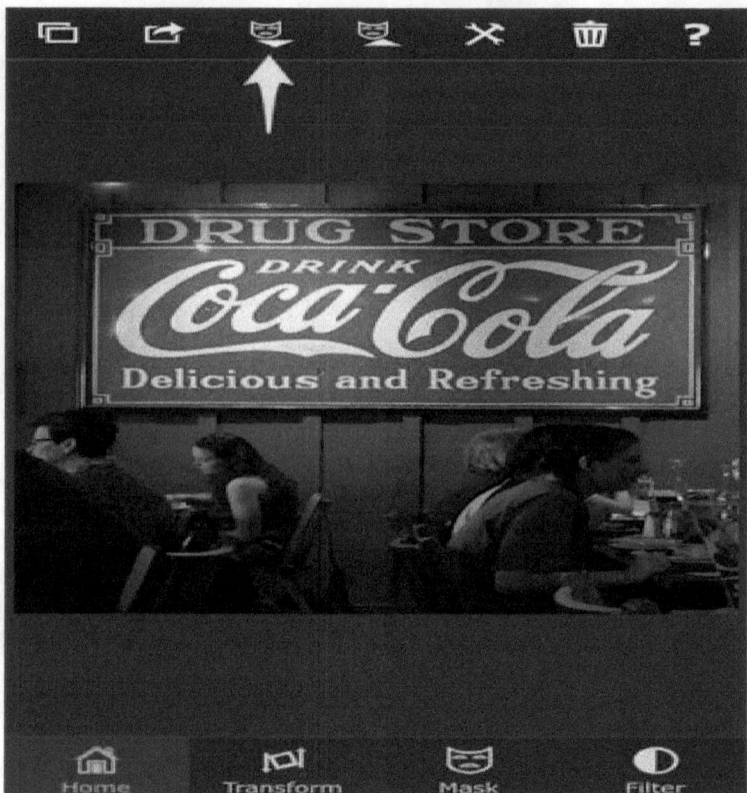

You'll now see the entire masks which you saved.

You can then Tap the masks you want to apply to place it onto your background image:

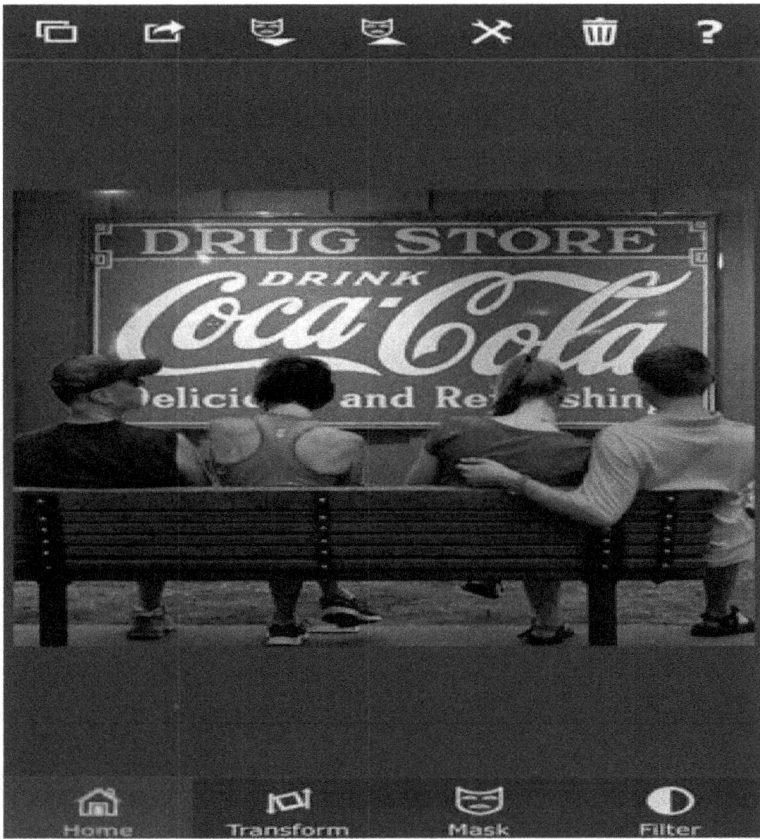

- **Save your Photo**

Whenever you're ready to save your final photograph, Tap the Export icon (second icon from the top left-hand side) in the Home section of the app. In the *Export Destination*, you can select photos to save the picture on your iPhone's photo library:

- **Delete the Session**

In case you choose to start the complete process again, Tap the Trash icon near the top of the display to delete the whole session to start afresh.

- **How to Produce a Double Exposure Picture**

Using the superimpose approach, you can also create

extraordinary increase exposure impact. This calls that you should mix two pictures instead of masking one of these.

It's quite easy to develop great portraits with **double exposure silhouettes** just as the example below:

That is likewise an advantageous way for including a **texture overlay** to your image which allows you to make a grunge look or textured painterly style. Here are the steps to check out to get this done;

Import Your Photographs

In the home portion of the superimpose app, use the import icon at the top right hand side to import your background and foreground photographs precisely as you did with the first approach described above.

As both pictures are imported, the foreground picture can

look similar to the background picture, as shown below:

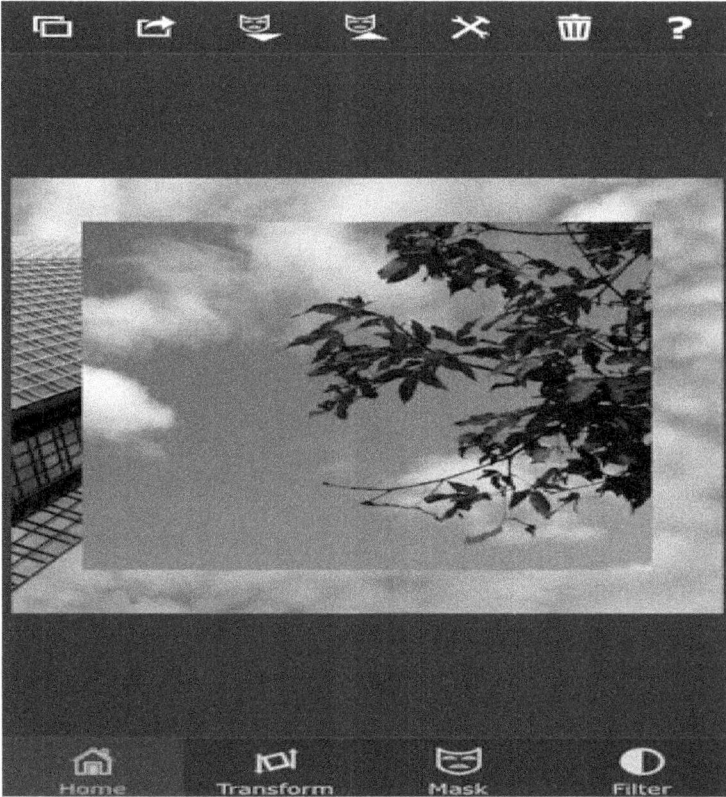

How to Blend the Pictures

You can start by Tapping the **Transform option** at the low area of the screen. This section is not limited by enabling you to reposition and resize your foreground picture; nonetheless, it additionally gives you access to change the transparency and mix mode.

To demand **Mix mode**, select the Settings icon at the very top right part of the display:

- **Mix mode** provides unique techniques; both pictures can also built-in together through the modification of presented tools such as comparison and brightness.

- The **Mix mode** is defined to default typically. It is one option to keep carefully the blend mode arranged to Normal and use the opacity slider to change the transparency of the foreground picture.

- Another approach is to see different blends of both pictures using a few of the other blend mode options, which consists of Multiply, Screen, Overlay, etc.

- You can merely Tap on the few different combination modes to observe how they have an impact on your final picture. Placing under consideration the example below, Overlay, Color, and Difference was used. Each one of these creates a unique and fantastic mixture of both pictures:

How to Change the Filter

- Tapping the Filter option in the bottom of the screen will enable you to apply a growth of preset filtration system results to beautify the image. There are also adjustment presented tools for *colour hue, saturation, exposure, brightness, comparison, colour balance, and blur.*

- You might use these results to each one of the foreground and background images. It's a step that isn't usually necessary, but it's a false choice to have.

- Near the top of the display, choose whether you want to focus on the foreground or background image. Just select the configurations icon at the very top right part of the screen, and also you'll visit a pass on of adjustment configurations you can use:

Moreover, within the Filter segment, Tap the **FX** icon to access 33 distinctive preset filters, as shown below:

You can effortlessly change the filter on either of the pictures or both, creating unlimited blend feasibilities. Below are some examples of double exposure image with distinctive filters implemented:

When you've completed the editing process of your photograph, you can return to the home section to save your picture.

Summarily; superimpose is a remarkable app for changing backgrounds of pictures, in addition to creating outstanding double exposure photos.

- All you have is a foreground image and a background image, and next use the superimpose software to masks and mix both pictures as you wish.

- Whenever you've actualized the *perfect blend*, don't neglect to check the filters and adjustment modifications to see when you can further improve your picture with distinct effects.

Once you have mastered the utilization of the superimpose app, after that, you can try advanced layer masking techniques. You can likewise make sure you browse the Leonardo App, which is a product of the same company. Leonardo helps several layers, a big group of image modifications, in addition to other editing and enhancing tools.

CHAPTER 8

iPhone Portrait Settings for Producing Perfect Blurry Background

The **iPhone portrait mode** is the correct device to make brilliant looking portrait photographs with your iPhone. Portrait setting gives you to quickly produce a shallow depth of field in your pictures. This leads to an excellent blurry background that could typically be performed with a **DSLR camera**. With this section, you'll see how to use the iPhone portrait setting to make a professional-looking iPhone photo with beautiful background blur.

What's Portrait Mode?

Portrait mode is a distinctive capturing mode available in the native camera application of an iPhone. It creates use of a unique **Depth Impact Tool** to make a shallow Depth of field in your pictures.

Shallow depth of field means that only a little area of the photo is within focus as the other is blurred. More often than not, you'll need your most significant concern at the mercy of appearing in razor-sharp focus as the background shows up blurred.

This soft and tender blurry background is categorized as "bokeh," which originates from the Japanese language.

Why should we use a Shallow Depth of Field?

The **shallow depth of Field** is often utilized by portrait photographers. Why? Since it places the focus on the average person and creates a sensitive, dreamy backdrop in it. Blurring the context is also truly useful when taking in locations with a busy, messy, or distracting backdrop. The blurring makes the context secondary, getting the viewer's attention back to the principal subject matter in the foreground.

Shallow Depth of Field isn't something you'd use for every kind of picture. You typically wouldn't want a blurry Background in scenery or architectural picture as you'd want to see everything vividly from foreground to Background.

However, in portrait pictures, a Shallow Depth of Field can make a significant distinction to the result of your photo. By blurring the backdrop, you may make your subject matter stand out.

How to Develop Background Blur Using an iPhone

Sometimes back, the iPhone camera hasn't allowed you to have any control over the depth of field for your pictures. You've had the choice to have everything in Focus - unless your most significant subject matter comes very near the zoom lens, in such case the backdrop seems blurred.

However, with portrait setting on the new iPhone, now you can pick and choose what's in focus and what isn't. This gives you unprecedented control over your iPhone camera, permitting you to mimic the appearance of DSLR cameras that can catch a shallow depth of field.

While portrait mode is most beneficial when planning on taking pictures of humans, pets, nature etc., it can be utilized to blur the backdrop behind any subject.

Many things appear better when there's a soft, dreamy background in it - especially if that background could distract the viewer from the primary subject.

How to use iPhone Portrait Mode

- Developing a shallow **Depth of Field** with Portrait mode on the iPhone is super easy. You can start by starting the default camera app, then swipe through the taking pictures modes (video, picture, etc.) until Portrait is highlighted in yellow.

- The very first thing you'll notice when you switch to Portrait Setting is that everything gets enlarged. That's because the camera automatically switches to the iPhone's 2x Telephoto Zoom lens. The telephoto zoom lens typically creates more flattering portrait images than the huge-angle zoom lens that could distort cosmetic features.

- You'll additionally spot the words **Depth Impact** appears in the bottom of the screen. Moreover, your telephone will help you giving on-screen instructions in case you don't have things framed up optimally for an enjoyable portrait shot. For instance, you'll possibly see Move Farther Away or even more Light Required:

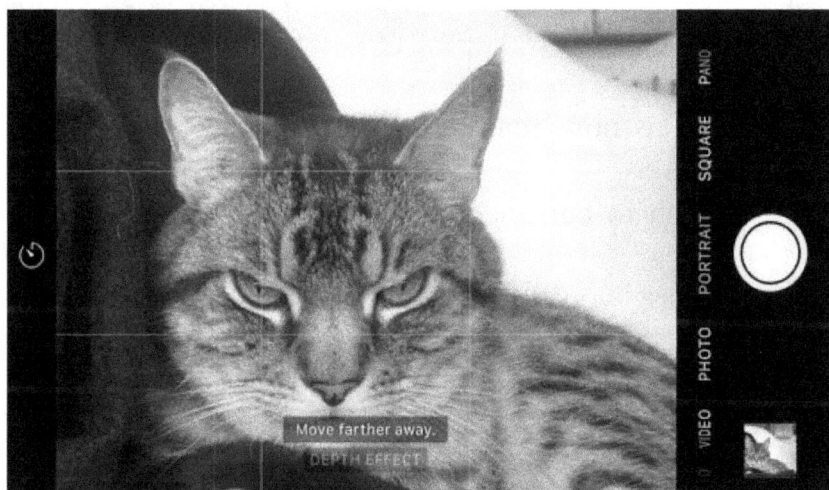

- The moment you're at the right distance from your subject, the words **Depth Effect** would be highlighted in yellow. You'll also see four yellow crop marks, indicating the face of your subject:

- You're now ready to take, so select the shutter button to consider your picture. After making the picture, you'll observe that two variations of the image can look in the camera app. One image will have the *Depth Impact* (blurred Background) and the other won't.

- Evaluating those two versions of the image sincerely suggests how nice a portrait picture shows up when it has a **Shallow Depth of Field**.

- If for reasons unknown you're not sure which of both pictures had the **Depth impact**, it'll be labelled in your image Set as shown below:

Tips For Creating Awesome Background Blur

When taking pictures with the iPhone portrait mode, it's essential to think about your background plus your subject. The type of Background you choose against its distance from your subject matter, will each have a significant effect on the final image.

The **Depth Effect** in Portrait mode is most effective when your subject matter is not the backdrop. The further away the topic is from the backdrop, the more delightful blur you'll get. Spot the difference in the backdrop blur of the two pictures:

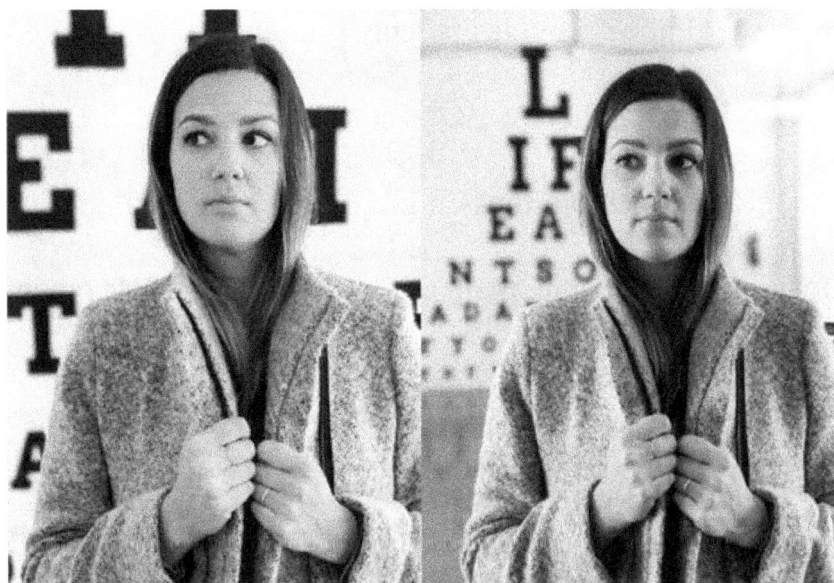

Subject close to background   Subject farther away from background

So; if your Background doesn't show up blurry enough when taking photos in a portrait setting, move your subject matter further from the background.

It's additionally essential to have something in the backdrop so that there are a few components for the camera to blur.

Conclusively; the iPhone has continuously been a first-rate device for most types of picture taking - such as landscape, structures, and street picture taking. However, now the iPhone provides potential to take amazing, high-quality portrait photos.

The telephoto zoom lens on the iPhone is more flattering for shooting people than the typical wide-angle zoom lens.

As well as the **Magical Depth Impact tool** in the iPhone Portrait Mode creates lovely background blur - simulating the shallow depth of field that could formerly only be performed with a DSLR camera.

Taking photos with the iPhone portrait mode is a delight.

Moreover, your subject will be thrilled when you suggest

to them how beautiful they show up on your photos.

Don't forget; even while Portrait mode is the perfect

setting when planning on taking pictures of individuals,

pets, nature, etc., you can use it on any subject matter in

which you require to make an attractive *background*

blur.

CHAPTER 9

Perfect Camera Apps for iPhone

Looking for the best camera application for an iPhone? Even while the default iPhone camera application has some fantastic capabilities, sometimes you'll want a more effective camera. However, with so many camera applications available online, it might be tough to discover which to use. This assessment of the five best iPhone camera applications will help you to find the right app for you.

VSCO: How to Use VSCO

You might already be familiar with the VSCO application as it's more popular because of its picture improving functions and beautiful movie-like filters.

However, this free application also has an effectively integrated camera with many guide settings.

- If you are capturing in VSCO, you could have manual control of *Focus, Exposure, White Stability*, as well as *ISO and Shutter Speed.* Depending on how new your iPhone is, you may even have the ability to shoot in *Natural Mode.*

- To gain access to the camera in VSCO, open up the application, and swipe down with your finger. Once you are in the camera setting, you'll see numerous icons underneath (or the medial side, if you're making use of your phone horizontally) which may enable you to customize the camera configurations.

However, the above are just a few of the customizable options. If you swipe on the icons with your finger, you'll see there are very a few extra "hiding" solely off display.

A significant number of the advanced camera features toggle among distinctive alternatives (flash, the grid, raw, and the funny "face overlay" choice), while some think of a slider for excellent fine-tuning settings with exposure, white balance, focus, iso, and shutter rate.

For example, if you select on the solar icon, the exposure slider will be observed at the lower part of the display screen as shown below.

- Pull the slider to change the exposure (brightness) of your picture. In case you want to return to the default automated exposure, select on the "A."

- The **White Balance (WB)** setting is utilized for actualizing the right colors on your pictures by either starting to warm up or trying to cool off the colors. Use the slider to change the color heat in your image.

- You can view below two variations of the same image - one with a more relaxed white balance setting (bluer) and one with a warmer white balance setting (more orange). The colour temp will have a significant effect on the overall temper of your picture.

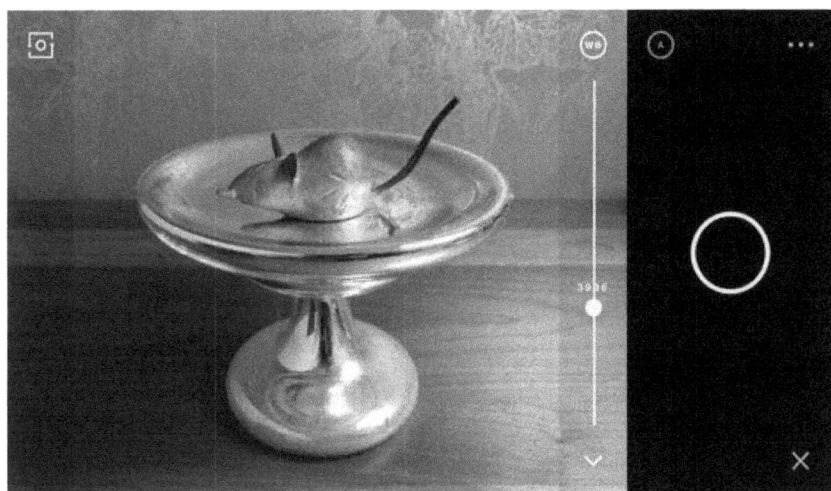

The ISO setting controls the digital camera's sensitivity to light, and for that reason affects the exposure (brightness) of the photograph. The better the ISO Volume, the brighter the exposure maybe. However, retain in mind that high ISO configurations can result in grainy images.

Shutter Speed settings the exposure time for the picture. Lengthy exposures are perfect for night picture taking, blurring movement, and taking light trails.

When capturing lengthy exposure images, be sure you hold the camera still actually to avoid any camera tremble that brings about blurry pictures. Make use of a tripod for the product quality results.

While you're dealing with those type of manual settings in VSCO, you're essentially making the utilization of your iPhone as if you would use a manual DSLR camera.

VSCO can be an excellent application to use if you're merely starting or a dummy by using third-party camera apps. It's available for download from the application store and has a great selection of manual handles that will put in a level of course and creativeness to your pictures.

MANUAL: How to Use Manual

- If manual camera settings are what you're after, the aptly named manual application ($3.99) is just about the best replacement camera application for your iPhone. Quickly, you can transform the Shutter Velocity, ISO, and exposure values to attain the creative impact you need.

- Unlike VSCO, you have the decision to manually control the camera settings, which include **Focus, White Balance, ISO, Shutter Rate,** and **brightness (*called EV*).**

- The interface is quite intuitive. When you release the app, all the configurations are in automated mode. If you wish to change to manual control, select and hold on to the ISO or Shutter Rate, and you'll be able to access your configurations. Moreover, if you would like to restore to the automated setting, Tap the "A."

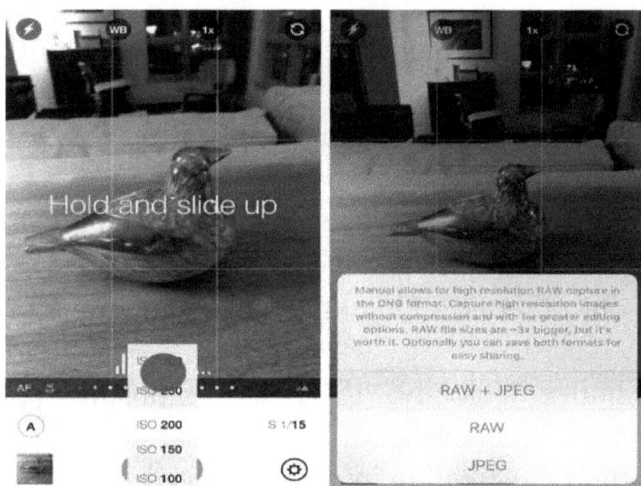

- You can even decide if you would like to snap images in Raw Layout, JPEG Layout, or both. Natural capture enables you to store images without compression, ensuring an excellent picture that provides you with more significant potential for improvement during editing. However, retain in mind that Natural photos take up plenty of more space for storage on your phone.

- There's a specific setting that may be great, which is the slow shutter velocity.

- Another superb feature of the manual application is that you can by hand Focus on your subject. Just slip your finger left or directly on the Focus bar at the lowest area of the screen till your subject matter sometimes appears in perfect Focus. If you wish to go back to the auto-focus setting, select the AF button.

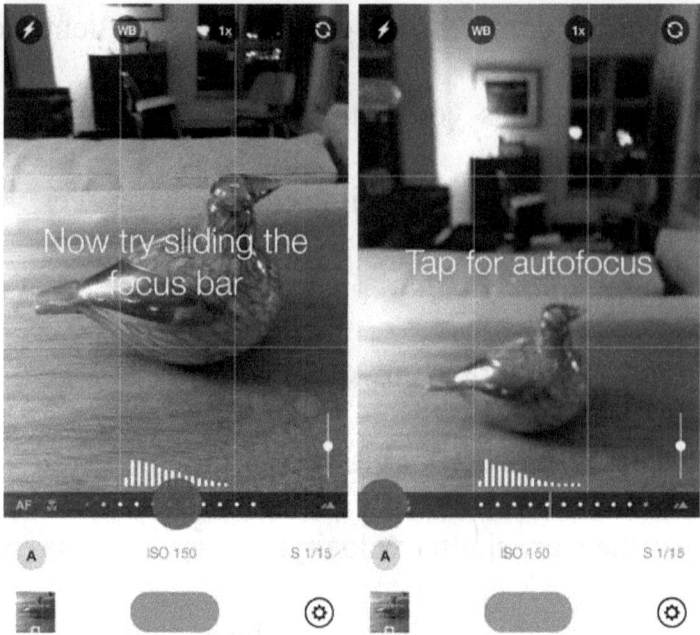

This app also offers a particular focusing device, rendering it more straightforward to focus manually. Once you start sliding the Focus bar, a middle square magnifies the subject, and that means you can test thoroughly your important Focus. This standard concentrating feature is particularly useful while taking up close or macro issues.

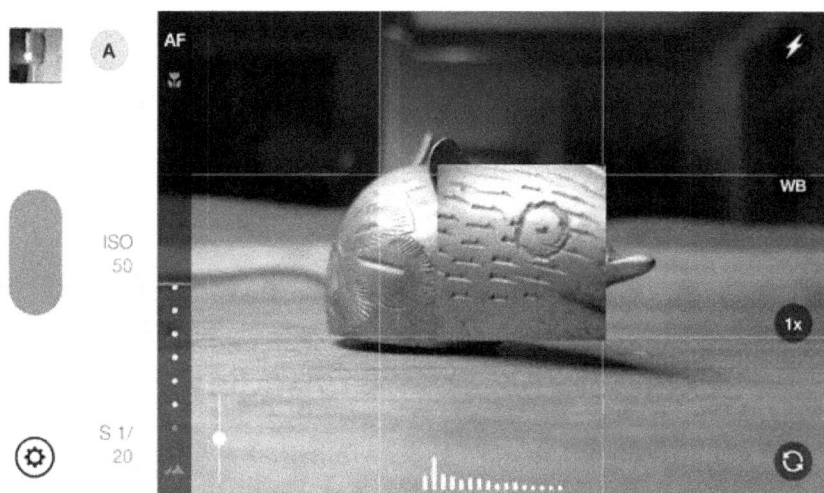

Having the ability to control those advanced manual settings provides you with more excellent alternatives as an iPhone photographer, letting you create the best feasible picture, even in complex taking conditions.

CAMERA+: How to Use Camera+

Camera+ is a superb camera and picture enhancing app combined. This is the first advanced camera app I've seen great photographers using on iPhone, and you may set the centre point, and exposure one following the other, as the timer for the camera, could be arranged for 30 mere seconds.

- The camera+ programmer has continued to enhance the app over time, and it's now stronger than ever. All the classic features are just like they were; nevertheless, you could now use digital camera+ much as if you use the manual app. You can even shoot in Natural mode and extra control of your last photograph.

- In camera+ it's the simplest. It is easy to switch the centre point, exposure, and white balance to creatively impact the feeling of your snap photos.

- To create the Focus and exposure individually, select on display with two fingertips at the same instant of your time. You'll visit an individual exposure factor (orange group) and Focus (red square). Pull the Focus and contact with distinctive elements of the picture until it appears the just as what you would like it to appear to be.

- If you wish to alter the shutter velocity and ISO configurations, Tap the group icon above the shutter release button. A -panel will slip up, letting you by hand change the configurations.

- The shutter speed setting appears on the left and the ISO at the right; swipe through each establishing to alternate them. To escape the manual configurations and came back to the default setting, you could either Tap the automated button or dual Tap the screen.

- Typically you will never need to disturb yourself about **white balance** because the iPhone does a notable activity of fabricating all the colourations to appear genuine. However, you can personally override the white balance placing to provide your photos with a different feel.

- You might use the shutter speed and ISO settings in camera+ to obtain computer images extraordinary impact evergreen exposures. In the example underneath, an image of a pool that experienced a lovely tree sculpture was captured.

The primary picture (above) converted into shot using the iPhone's default camera app. It made an appearance pretty good; nevertheless, the reflections and ripples in the water had been some distraction.

So let look at case research where the camera+ is utilized to shoot an extended exposure of the picture as shown below. You will observe how the sluggish shutter velocity has made water show up silky smooth. This makes the water significantly less distracting, and on the other hand, your vision is attracted to the tree.

Underneath you might observe how this impact in digital camera+. Indeed, when you have an iPhone, or later versions would be, digital camera+ will continue to work with either of the telephone's lens. Because of this shot, it was turned to the telephoto zoom lens (group icon near to top left) because the photographer couldn't get near to the tree without getting damp!

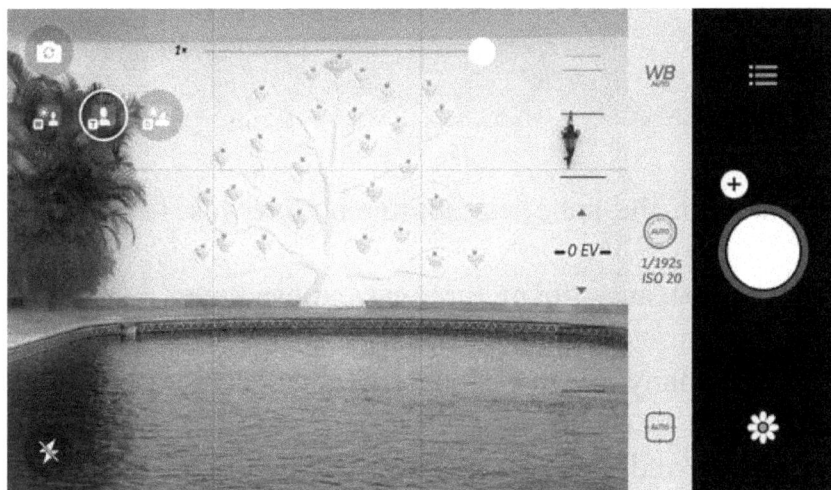

Moreover, subsequently, Tap the automatic button to show the manual controls. The shutter speed was set to an entirely long 8 seconds (with the iPhone set up on a tripod) and reduced the ISO value as little as reasonable (which on camera+ was 0.01) to make sure the photo didn't end up over-exposed (too brilliantly bright).

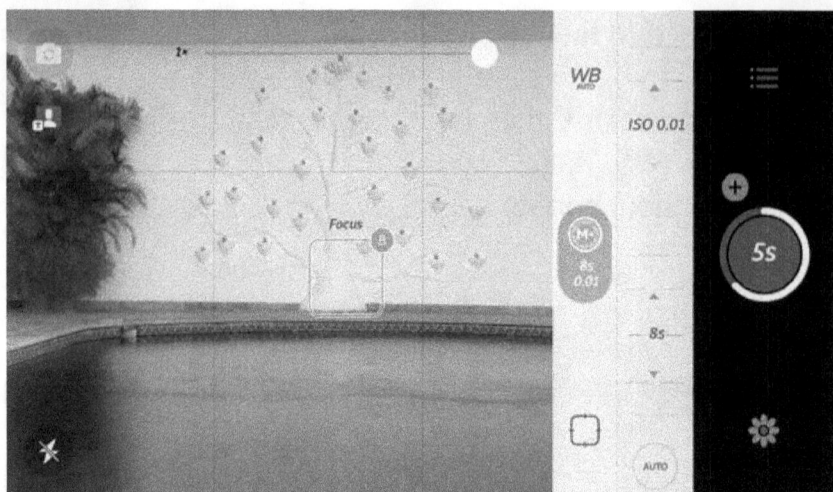

In the end, the spherical shutter button was Tapped and watched because the picture was exposed over 8 seconds. Among many of these camera apps, camera+ is very powerful and can be a bit overwhelming. So I will recommend that you attempt out one function at a time and get accustomed to it before moving on to the next.

ProCAMERA: How to Use ProCAMERA

The ProCamera app, especially the latest version, gives you a remarkable number of control over your settings while taking pictures.

- Asides the usual manual controls like shutter speed, ISO and white balance, the application also includes advanced features like **RAW capture**, a **live histogram**, an **anti-shake feature**, and the capability to access either camera lens in the iPhone or later version of iPhone such as iPhone 11, iPhone XS, iPhone XR, etc.

- In case you're shooting in low light (or with the telephoto zoom lens, when camera shake is more of a threat) and you don't have a tripod, attempt shooting with the use of the anti-shake mode.

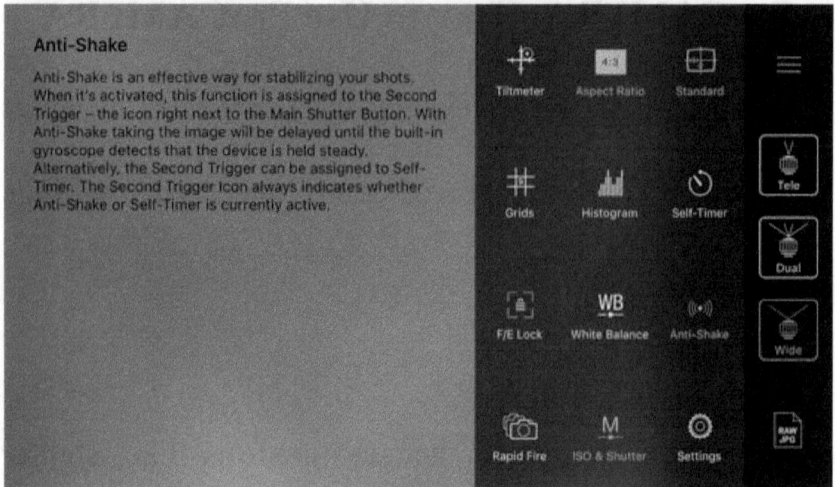

Anti-Shake

Anti-Shake is an effective way for stabilizing your shots. When it's activated, this function is assigned to the Second Trigger – the icon right next to the Main Shutter Button. With Anti-Shake taking the image will be delayed until the built-in gyroscope detects that the device is held steady. Alternatively, the Second Trigger can be assigned to Self-Timer. The Second Trigger Icon always indicates whether Anti-Shake or Self-Timer is currently active.

Tiltmeter   Aspect Ratio   Standard

Grids   Histogram   Self-Timer   Tele

F/E Lock   White Balance   Anti-Shake   Dual

Rapid Fire   ISO & Shutter   Settings   Wide

- This mode uses your iPhone's integrated intervalometer to gauge how much the telephone is moving. After that, it waits till you're securing to the camera at a sharp point before it requires a photo. That is a significant-excellent characteristic!

Once you want to modify shutter velocity and ISO, you have options. The first option is by using a fully manual setting where you control both *ISO and Shutter Velocity*.

Manual Mode

In Manual Mode you have the option to dial in specific values for exposure time and ISO value. To change the current values, simply tap the corresponding ISO number or exposure time at the top of the screen. Tap the M icon again to toggle between the two other modes: Semi-Automatic Mode (SI) and Automatic Mode (M icon is white).

Tiltmeter   Aspect Ratio   Standard

Grids   Histogram   Self-Timer   Tele

Dual

F/E Lock   White Balance   Anti-Shake   Wide

Rapid Fire   ISO & Shutter   Settings

- The task with manual mode is you need to balance the shutter speed, and ISO settings is to be sure you get the exposure accurate (not too darkish not too shiny). In the event you're not used to the use of the settings, you will get this complicated to get right.

- Therefore, the second choice is to make by using **SI mode**, which enables you to change either the Shutter Speed or the ISO, and the application

209

adjusts the choice establishing to calculate the perfect exposure. This setting is exceptional if you're not used to the utilization of manual exposure settings.

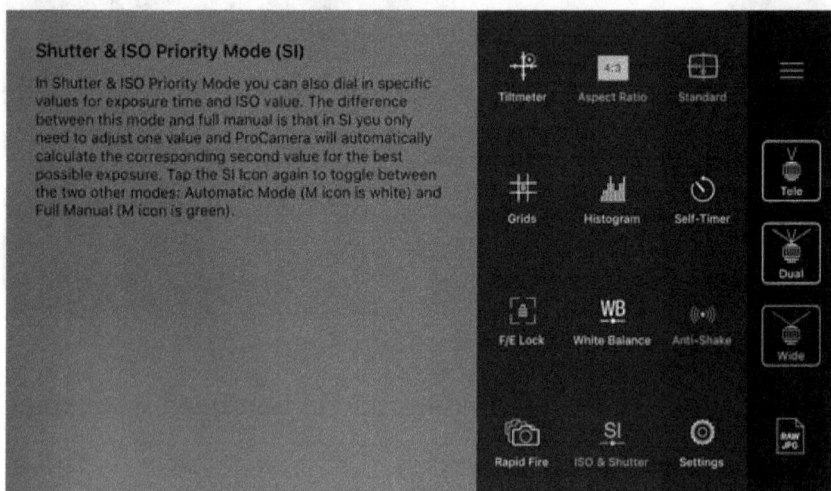

Shutter & ISO Priority Mode (SI)

In Shutter & ISO Priority Mode you can also dial in specific values for exposure time and ISO value. The difference between this mode and full manual is that in SI you only need to adjust one value and ProCamera will automatically calculate the corresponding second value for the best possible exposure. Tap the SI icon again to toggle between the two other modes: Automatic Mode (M icon is white) and Full Manual (M icon is green).

ProCamera additionally can customize the self-timer for any amount of time as much as 30 seconds. This is very beneficial.

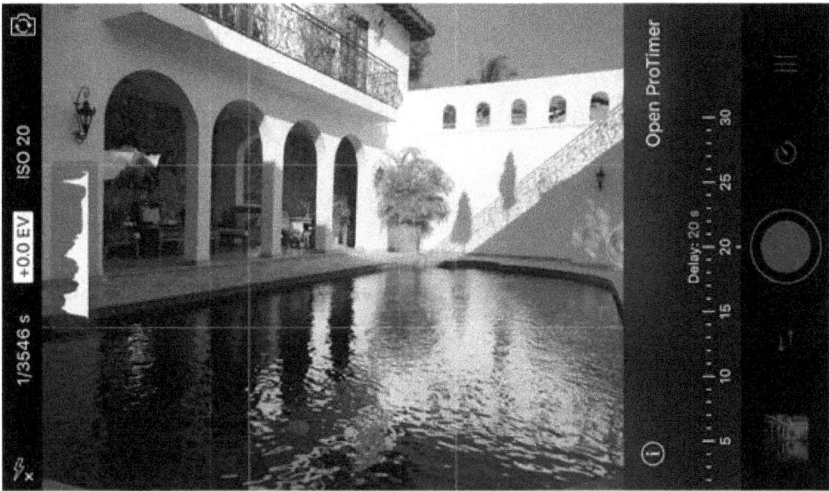

For this image, the iPhone was set on a tripod, then set the timer delay to 20 seconds to provide sufficient time to walk into the shot for the photographer to be seen in the photograph.

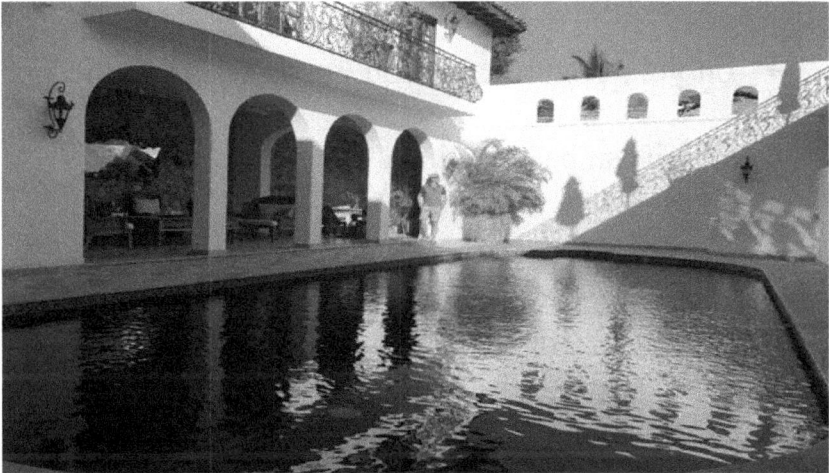

- Another great function of the self-timer would be that the flash blinks each second until it requires the picture. This implies you don't need to be surprised at how time has exceeded and set up picture has been used. After the blinking halts, you'll know you can get back to the iPhone to indeed have a look at your shot.

- Finally, there are a variety of in-app purchases you may make if you want to try their HDR or low-light cameras. You can get from them a free trial to see what they do; however, you'll get a watermark on your picture until you purchase the application which can be an optional setting available.

Cortex Cam: How to Use Cortex Cam

Cortex Cam is one of the applications which makes you

scrape your mind in amazement the very first time you operate it!

- The magic of cortex cam is it lets you take in low, moderate conditions and take long exposures without needing a tripod. Think about this for a second. You may take a picture where the exposure lasts for many seconds without having to apply a tripod. It's amazing!

- Just how cortex cam works is that whenever you Tap the shutter button, the application takes a large number of snapshots and traces them up to eliminate any camera movement from your shaky hands. It eventually merges them into a single photo.

- The resulting picture is sharp, though it became shot handheld. Low slight images frequently tend to have plenty of digital sounds (grain) that may damage the grade of the picture, but cortex cam creates very low-noise pictures. I take benefit of this app each time I'm capturing during the night time.

- You can additionally use cortex cam in the daylight for long exposure photos of water, and many more. In the example below the application was used to smoothen stream in the pool, to give picture a special feeling.

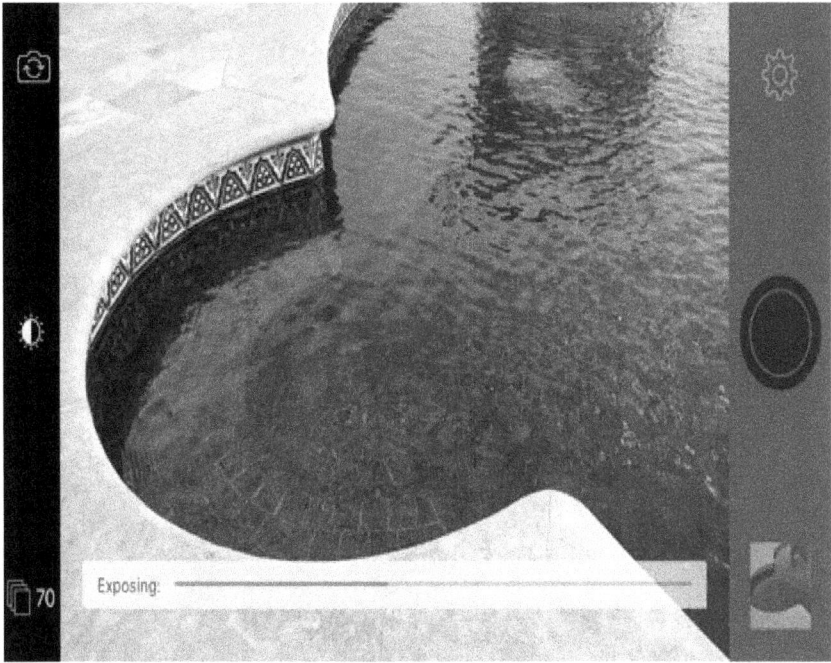

The cease final result is shown below. This may have been a created impact by using a sluggish shutter speed environment in virtually any other camera app, but I'd experienced to employ a tripod. Cortex allows developing a protracted exposure water picture while hand-holding an iPhone.

Third-party iPhone camera applications are mind-boggling. There are some features to take into account and many apps to choose from.

The five iPhone camera applications that we've explored in this book will be the high-quality applications obtainable. If you want great control of camera configurations and creativeness, you should certainly begin with these explained apps.

Although each one of these apps has plenty of comparable features, each of them works in slightly different approaches and show unique user interfaces. To look for the best iPhone camera application for you is dependent wholly on finding which features and user interface you desire.

I would suggest you start with the free VSCO app, merely to get accustomed to the thought of controlling lots of more superior camera features. Then if you find which application you want for higher control, try a couple of the other apps - manual, digital camera+ or ProCamera - offering exposure, white balance, ISO and shutter velocity settings.

If you likewise need to take handheld during the night time, or you want to capture lengthy exposure pictures without the utilization of the tripod, you certainly can't beat Cortex Cam.

NB: *It's not essential to own many of these apps, as many of them are pretty comparable. I'll endorse learning the set of features for each of this software on the App Store, and next select just one which meets your needs or goes for whatever provides the configurations beautiful for you.*

CHAPTER 10

How to Proceed When You Can't Activate Used iPhone

If you buy a used iPhone, it is interesting. In the end, you come with an iPhone and stretch your budget by acquiring a used one, especially for individuals who are not economically buoyant.

Some individuals encounter this issue along the way of activating their new device: The iPhone will inquire further for somebody else's Apple ID and wouldn't typically work unless supplied.

This isn't a challenge that can't be fixed, so do not fret because you'll get it fixed following these steps.

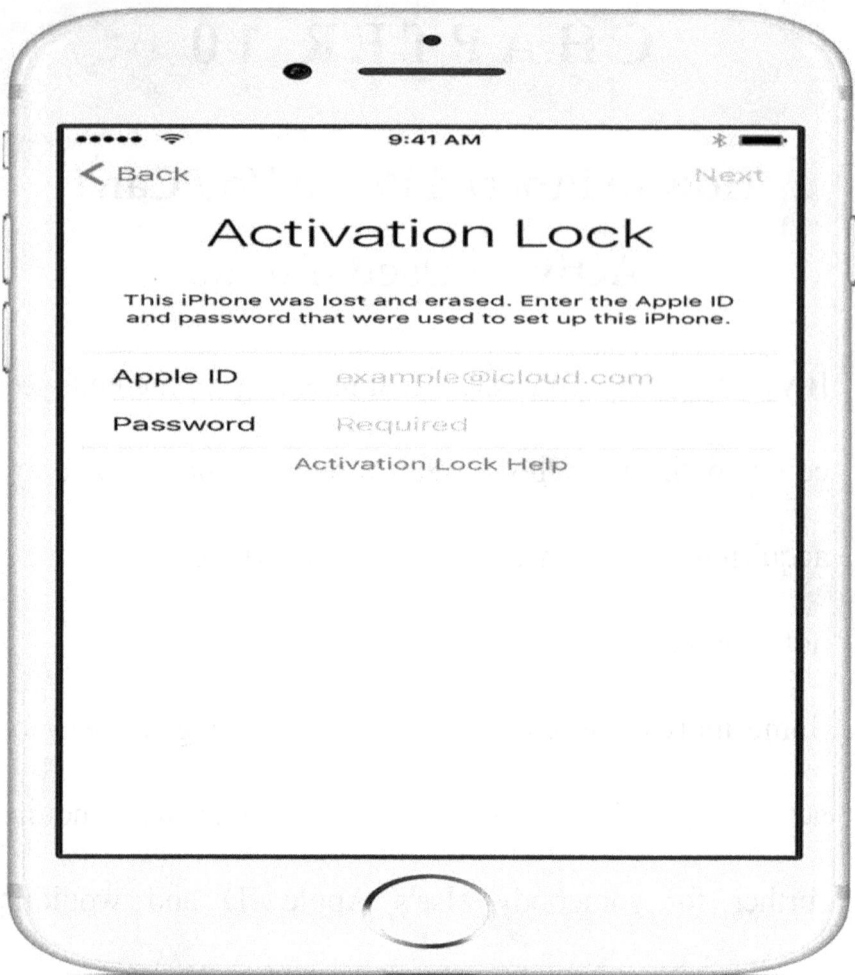

Activation Lock

This iPhone was lost and erased. Enter the Apple ID and password that were used to set up this iPhone.

Apple ID   example@icloud.com

Password   Required

Activation Lock Help

- It is consequently an attribute of Apple's Find my iPhone service known as activation lock.

- Activation Lock is a security measure that Apple

raised to cope with the allergy of iPhone thefts. In earlier years, if someone takes an iPhone without blockage by lock feature, they could clean it, resell it, and breakout with the crime. Activation lock altered the situation.

- When the initial owner setup finds my iPhone on the tool, the **Apple ID** used will be stored on Apple's activation servers together with almost every other information about the phone. The activation servers will most effectively unlock the phone again if that unique Apple ID can be used. If you no more have the Apple ID, you'll never be in a position to activate or use the phone. This facilitates the security of your iPhone because nobody would like to grab a phone they can't use. On the other hand, it generally does not harm you if you recently procure the phone.

- Dealing with activation lock is annoying, but additionally, it is smooth to solve. It's mainly possible, and the prior consumer just forgot to carefully turn off find my iPhone or erase the tool correctly before offering it on the market (though it could also be a sign you've purchased a stolen device, so be cautious).

- You should contact the preceding owner of the telephone for him/her to consider the necessary steps.

How to Remove Activation Lock on iPhone

- It is expedient that you should unlock or remove activation lock from the acquired iPhone (used iPhone) by inputting the prior owners' **Apple ID.** This technique can be initiated by getting in

contact with the owner and detailing the scenario.

- If the owner lives near to you, I'll recommend that you hand over the phone back to him/her with the mission to insert the mandatory unlock code which is his/her Apple ID. When the seller gets the iPhone at hand, he/she only will enter the necessary Apple ID on the activation lock display. Having done such, restart the telephone and then forge forward with the typical activation process.

Ways to Remove Activation Lock using iCloud

Sometimes, things can get a bit messy and complicated if the merchant/seller cannot physically access the phone thanks to circumstances such as distance among other factors. This may also be resolved effortlessly as the owner may use iCloud to eliminate the activation lock from the phone through his accounts by following the steps below:

- Visit iCloud.com on any device, either mobile or laptop.

- Log-on with the Apple ID he/she used to activate the telephone.

- Click Find My iPhone.

- Select All Devices.

- Go through the iPhone you sold or want to market.

- Select **Remove from Accounts.**

Having achieved that, after that, you can PULL THE PLUG ON the iPhone, and you switch it ON again. After that, you can proceed with the standard activation process.

How to Fix Locked Home-Screen or Security Password

If you activate your phone and find out either the iPhone's home display screen or the security password lock display, therefore that the supplier/vendor didn't completely erase the smartphone before offering it for you. On this notice, you'll need the owner to wipe these devices to be able to do it with the activation process.

The next two procedures should be followed as you hand over the phone to the owner or seller to unlock the phone;

- If the phone works on iOS 10 and later version, the owner has to log out of iCloud and subsequently erase these devices by heading *to Settings -> General -> reset -> Erase All Content* and *Settings.*

- If the phone works on iOS 9, the seller/seller must go to *Settings -> General -> reset -> Erase All*

Content and *Settings* and enter his/her Apple ID when prompted.

- When the erase process is completed, you're absolving to activate your phone with no further ado or hold off.

How to Wipe an iPhone Using iCloud

Imagine if you can't gain access to the vendor/merchant due to some reasons, yet you will need your mobile phone to be wiped entirely for easy convenience, the seller may use iCloud to erase it. This is attained by ensuring the phone you want to get triggered linked to a WiFi network or mobile data network, and then inform the seller to follow along with the next steps:

- Visit *iCloud.com/#find.*

- Sign in with the Apple id he/she applied to the phone that is with you or sold to you.

- Click *All Devices*.

- Choose the phone sold you or available to you.

- Select *Erase iPhone*.

- When the phone is erased, click *Remove from Accounts*.

- Restart the phone, and you are all set.

How to Erase an iPhone Using Find My iPhone App

This process is very much indeed identical to the approach explained above using iCloud by just using the Find my iPhone application installed on some other iPhone device. If the owner prefers to get this done, connect the phone you're buying to Wi-Fi or mobile data, and then inform the owner to adhere to the steps below:

- Start the *find my iPhone* app.

- Sign on with the Apple ID they applied to the phone sold
  to you.

- Choose the phone.

- Tap *Actions*.

- Tap *Erase iPhone*.

- Tap *Erase iPhone* (It is the same button, however on a
  new display).

- Enter *Apple ID*.

- Tap *Erase*.

- Tap *Remove from Accounts*.

Restart the iPhone and get started doing the setup
process.

CHAPTER 11

Steps for Fixing an iPhone Power Problems

Sometimes whenever your iPhone doesn't start, you will think you should buy a new phone. This can be true if the trouble is terrible enough; however, there are diverse methods to be applied on your iPhone before you finally conclude that the phone is dead. In case your iPhone doesn't **START**, try these six steps to get the problem set yourself.

- **Charge Your Phone**

Ensure that your iPhone's battery is well charged sufficiently to power the smartphone.

If you wish to try this, plug your iPhone into a wall structure charger or your personal computer via USB cable, but I strictly recommend using power. Make sure you allow it charge for at least fifteen to thirty minutes. This could make your mobile phone get start up automatically, or you can also press down the power button to carefully turn it ON.

If regardless you think your phone ran out of battery when using or recharging fails, it is feasible that your charger or cable is defective or the battery is terrible which implies you may want to acquire another battery. You can try to use various other cables to check.

- **Restart Your iPhone**

If charging the battery didn't Turn your iPhone ON or your iPhone does not charge while ON and you're sure the charger works on other mobile phones, the next thing you have to try is to restart the phone. This is attained by pressing down the **power button** at the very top right side of the smartphone for a couple of seconds. If the smartphone is OFF, it must turn ON. If it's ON, you will notice the slider offering to turn it OFF.

- **Hard Reset the iPhone**

You could attempt a hard reset if the normal restart didn't transform it ON. A hard reset is kind of a restart that clears a higher percentage of the phone's memory space (however not its storage space, you won't lose any document) for a more complete reset.

Follow the below instructions to apply hard reset:

1. Press and hold down the **Power Button** and **Home Button** at the same time. (If you work with the iPhone 7 and later versions, Press down **Power** and **Volume Button** at the same time.)

2. Maintain holding down those button for at least ten

seconds (there is certainly nothing at all absurd with holding those button down for 20 or 30 secs, however, if nothing at all has occurred by holding them down, it in all probability won't work)

3. If the Shut-down slider shows up on the screen, maintain pressing the buttons

4. Until when the white Apple logo design appears, after that, you can remove your hands off those buttons and allow phone start up.

5. Restore iPhone to Factory Settings.

Sometimes the best strategy is restoring your iPhone to its production default settings. This technique will remove all the info and configurations on your phone (You can synchronize and backup your details), and in exchange fix a significant number of problems.

Although typically, you'll synchronize your iPhone and restore it using iTunes, however, if your iPhone won't activate, try these steps:

1.   Plugin the iPhone's **USB cable** to the connection slot, yet not into your personal computer.

2.   Press down the iPhone's **Home button** (while on an iPhone 7 or later version, press down **Volume button**).

3.   While still pressing down the home button, plug the contrary end of the USB wire into your personal computer.

4.   This will result in opening **iTunes**, it'll automatically place the iPhone into recovery setting, and consequently, help you completely restore the iPhone.

- **Put iPhone into DFU Mode**

In a few situations, your iPhone might not get **Started** as it does not boot up. This may happen after jailbreaking the phone or when you try to install an iOS revise without enough space for storage or battery life.

If this is the problem you're facing, you can simply put your mobile phone in **DFU Mode** by following these processes:

1.   Plug your iPhone into your personal computer.

2.   Please press down the **Power button** for three mere seconds, then allow it to be.

3.   Press down the **Power button** and the **Home button** (with an iPhone 7 or later versions, press **Volume down**) together for approximately 10 seconds.

4.   Release your hands from the **Power button**, however, maintain pressing down the home button (with an iPhone 7 or later versions, keep the volume down) for about 5 seconds.

5.   If the screen remains dark and nothing appears noticeable, you're in **DFU Mode**. Adhere to the onscreen instructions in iTunes.

- **Reset Proximity Sensor**

There is undoubtedly another situation that can make your iPhone never to turn **ON,** which is a defect in the proximity sensor that dims the iPhone's display screen. This causes the screen to remain darkish even if the smartphone is **ON** rather than also near to your face.

Follow the instructions highlighted below;

1.   Press down the home and **Power Button** to restart the phone.

2.   When it restarts, the screen should then be working.

3.   Tap the **Configurations app.**

4.   Tap **General.**

5.   Tap **Reset.**

6.   Tap **Reset All Configurations**. This will erase all your preferences and configurations on the iPhone, however, won't delete your data.

If regardless your iPhone won't start after these steps; the problem is most likely too severe to revive personally. I would suggest you contact Apple support. The support staff will either repair your phone or let you know what it could cost to fix the problem.

You should check the status of your iPhone's warranty before going to the repair center because that could save you additional money on the repair.

www.ingramcontent.com/pod-product-compliance
Lightning Source LLC
Chambersburg PA
CBHW071201210326
41597CB00016B/1631